ORGANIZE YOUR BUSINESS TRAVEL!

SIMPLE WAYS TO MANAGE YOUR WORK WHILE YOU'RE OUT OF THE OFFICE

ORGANIZE YOUR BUSINESS TRAVEL!

SIMPLE WAYS TO
MANAGE YOUR WORK WHILE
YOU'RE OUT OF THE OFFICE

RONNI EISENBERG WITH KATE KELLY

HYPERION

NEW YORK

Library of Congress Cataloging-in-Publication Data

Eisenberg, Ronni.
Organize your business travel! : simple ways to manage your work while you're
out of the office / Ronnie Eisenberg with Kate Kelly.
p.   cm.
ISBN 0-7868-8626-9
1. Office practice. 2. Business travel. I. Kelly, Kate. II. Title.
HF5547 .E46   2001
651.3—dc21   00-047104

First Edition

10 9 8 7 6 5 4 3 2 1

CONTENTS

INTRODUCTION

No matter how you feel about business travel, this book will help you. The person who doesn't mind traveling for business but feels disorganized will gather lots of suggestions; the person who dislikes traveling for work because of the toll it takes on his or her personal life will be able to enjoy traveling more by learning how to manage better both at home and while away.

Your feelings about business travel depend upon who you are. *American Demographics* magazine reported on a study conducted for Hyatt Hotels, and while eight out of ten business travelers said that working on the road is stressful, most felt that it wasn't overly so. Some like the break in routine and the sense of adventure; those who enjoy it less are those who are concerned about their situation at home.

Understandably, business travel is hardest on workers with young families. Workers with steady partners are less likely to complain that travel detracts from their family life, perhaps partly because their spouse or significant other may be free to join them for a long weekend now and then. Being single is no "solution" to the perfect travel life—the unmarrieds worry because they have no one to feed the cat or pay the bills, and they worry about losing touch with friends at home.

Whatever your status, when you pick up your briefcase and suitcase and go out the door, one thing is abundantly clear. There are two main elements to making business travel work:

1. **Organization.** Whether you're out of the office for an hour, a day, a week, or a month, you'll read countless tips on how to stay organized at home and on the road. You'll find that some of the most tiresome aspects of travel are now quite manageable because you're organized.

2. **Attitude.** Throughout the book you'll hear from road warriors who actually don't mind traveling because they view business travel with a spirit of adventure and see it as an opportunity to see parts of the country or the world they never would have visited otherwise. They also like meeting people who introduce them to everything from new and interesting business concepts to terrific restaurants in their hometowns.

You may want to read this book straight through so you don't miss any good ideas, or you may prefer to skip around and read about the subjects that interest you most.

With this book as your guide, you'll find that you can enjoy your business travel time with less stress and more ease. From seeing new sights and meeting new people to maintaining time for yourself while away, you may discover that your work life is actually more enjoyable because you get to travel.

PART ONE

GETTING

READY

1

GETTING OUT OF THE OFFICE

AND MANAGING IT WHILE YOU'RE AWAY

WHAT'S AHEAD

Planning Is Key
Your Travel Files
Your Itinerary
Mail and Messages
Staff Management

etting out of the office for a business trip can be as difficult as extracting your feet from quicksand. The phone doesn't stop ringing, everyone on your staff seems to need you, and the incoming e-mail messages keep coming. In the meantime, you're trying to pull together sales material or presentation items, speech notes, or client documents in order to operate efficiently while you're away. Getting away is never easy!

The systems you implement for the time you're away should help make your departure easier and provide your staff with the information they need to manage while you're gone. The suggestions offered here should smooth out any kinks in your current system and help ease your preparation for your next trip as well as all those in the future.

PLANNING IS KEY

If you possibly can, try to plan out your travel schedule six months in advance. While some people work in fields where they must travel "as needed" and can't plan very far ahead, most people should be able to chart out on a calendar a very close estimate of when they must be gone.

When planning your long-range travel schedule, do so with both your office schedule and a full list of upcoming personal dates. If you have to schedule a trip in May or June you'll want to know when the dance recitals and end-of-school events are so, if possible, you can plan around them.

Both you and your staff will benefit if you can plan ahead on the timing of your business travel.

YOUR TRAVEL FILES

When it's time to travel, two types of files will come in very handy:

Destination Files: These files should be devoted to the cities you're visiting on upcoming business trips. For any city you visit regularly, create a permanent file where you keep maps, lists of favorite restaurants, great meeting spots, names and addresses of office service companies (couriers, quick print shops, limo companies, etc.), museums, and other local names and numbers you'd like to have whenever you visit. A convention in New Orleans for a one-time visit merits the creation of a temporary New Orleans file where you can keep all the information you gather about visiting New Orleans, including hotel and restaurant recommendations and tourist attractions you'd like to see if you have time.

"Work To Go" Files: As you gather your "work to go" files, there are three possible categories:

1. *The Reason-You're-Going Work:* Papers and information related to the convention or client meetings that are the reason for the trip.

2. *Other Projects:* Work you need to do while away is a second category of files. If you've got a major presentation upon your return, then you may want to work on your speech while away. Or if you know that you have two completely free afternoons over the course of a five-day convention, take along specific projects to work on during that time. Out-of-office work time, when you're less likely to be interrupted, is truly golden. (There are no interruptions!)

   "Just in case" files may also need to go with you. If there is an ongoing or outstanding issue with a major client and the client or your staff may need your opinion on something, take the file—or part of the file—with you. To avoid carrying extra bulk, keep this category to a minimum, and if the documents to which you might need to refer can be e-mailed or faxed to you, don't pack them.

3. *Your On-the-Go Reading File:* Travel generally offers a fabulous opportunity to catch up on reading, and this is a file I recommend in all my organizing books. The file itself is designed to hold all the items that you pick up or receive in the mail but don't have time to read. Take all magazines and torn-out articles that

you think you'll be able to get through and then attack the stack with serious ambition while away. Returning with a much thinner file is also very rewarding!

- Create separate file folders for Work to Go categories for upcoming trips, and then add information to them over time.

- When traveling with client files, weed through and carry only what is relevant to the upcoming meeting. If you've had a long-term relationship with a client or have done a number of jobs for them, the full file could be quite thick, weighing you down with paperwork that you don't need to have with you.

- Completed work can be sent back to the office by overnight mail or placed in a Work Completed file you carry with you.

YOUR ITINERARY

- You or a staff member must create an itinerary that will guide you through all the logistics of your trip but also provide family and co-workers with information on your whereabouts at all times. A good itinerary starts by outlining all the travel arrangements (complete with airline phone numbers, car service details, and phone numbers, etc.), the hotel address and phone number and reservation name, and continues with an outline of your daily activities as well as contact information. The itinerary should note the time zone you're visiting.

- One businessperson, who often doesn't take her laptop computer on short overnight trips, takes the itinerary sheet a step further and has her assistant create index cards with the information she needs. "The first index card provides me with all flight information, including backup flights if mine is cancelled or delayed. The appointment cards list the name, address, and phone number for each person to be visited. I like the system because a quick peek at the card provides a blueprint for what I'm to do next," she says. "I use the back of the card to record expenses related to the visit as well as make notations for follow-up. When I get back to my hotel room, a quick flip through the cards gives me items for my Master 'To Do' List. Then I band up the cards for each trip and have complete documentation of my expenses if I ever need them."

- Your office (boss and assistant), your family, and any good friends, including those who are watching your home or caring for your pets, should all receive a copy of your itinerary.

MAIL AND MESSAGES

- Arrange for a member of your staff to sort through your mail. If you're gone for more than three days, priority items should be sent to you by overnight mail. (For three-day trips, you may want the mail delivered to your home so that you can go through it quickly before your first day back at work.) Many businesspeople request that all but junk mail be sent. "I want my industry publications sent to me on the road," says one businessman. "There may be an article that is relevant to an issue I'm handling, and I certainly want to read through those publications before my return. It would ruin my first day back in the office if those stacks of magazines and newspapers were held for me."

- If you're gone until the weekend, have Friday's mail sent overnight to your home. (Make certain it's clearly marked for Saturday delivery.) So that you aren't trapped at home waiting for a delivery, check off the box indicating that no signature is required. That way the package can be left without you being there. The person who sends the package to you should fax you the airbill or e-mail you the tracking number in case the package is late or lost. With that information you can conduct the tracking process online.

- Unless you are checking e-mail as regularly as you do when in your own office, set your e-mail program to generate an automatic reply so that people understand why they haven't heard from you. Your automatic reply could indicate that you're away but you'll catch up with your e-mail later in the day, or it could indicate that you are out of communication until your return.

- Change your voice mail message to indicate the length of your absence and/or how else to reach you. It's far more efficient for people to learn that you are out of the office so they aren't stuck waiting for a reply.

- Make sure someone is checking your phone messages. Your secretary or assistant should handle anything he or she can; messages regarding more difficult issues should be archived so that you can listen to them yourself later.

- Establish a time when you will check in with the office each day. While business may dictate that you have to be in touch earlier than that, it provides your staff with the knowledge that no matter what, they will hear from you before the end of the day.

STAFF MANAGEMENT

Your absence will affect those who report to you in one of two ways: Some will have more to do, covering for you during your absence, and a few may actually have less to do if you're not there generating work.

Here's what you need to do so that no one is overwhelmed by too much work or too much free time:

- Delegate thoughtfully. You may have the best assistant in the world, but he or she should not have to work alone to fill the gap created by your absence. Meet with your assistant and discuss what tasks could be accomplished by others so that he or she can have more time to spend managing the priority issues that arise in your absence.

- Training is an important part of delegating. If another staff member is absorbing a new task because of your absence, print out instructions, but also arrange for you or an assistant to demonstrate and supervise the new tasks.

- Routine tasks should be described in step-by-step instructions for staff members to follow. You or a staff member should enter this information on the computer so that updates can be accomplished easily.

- If you have staff members who may actually have less to do because you are gone, create a permanent file where you toss notes about projects you'd like undertaken when you're away. You may have files that need to be sorted, mailing lists that need to be put onto the computer, scanning of documents, or any number of projects that could be accomplished when you're not there to generate work.

- Keep a list of what you've delegated. That way when you call in or once you've returned to the office, you'll have an organized way of following up.

YOUR BOSS

- Check with your boss about any ongoing projects. Does he or she need a person from your staff assigned to be on top of anything while you're gone? Is there anything he or she feels you should put on your own "To Do" List while you're conducting business away?
- Check in regularly. Out of town should not mean out of touch when it comes to your direct supervisor.

OFFICE DEPARTURE PREP

- Ship manuals, presentation information, or anything else that is bulky and plan for it to arrive a day ahead of you. Your assistant should follow up to confirm arrival. If something does happen to it, then you have the time to implement a backup plan and carry the materials with you if you have to.

- If you're going to be out of touch for a prolonged period, warn clients of this several days in advance. This provides them with the opportunity to talk to you before your departure, but it should save you some of the grief of hearing from everyone on the last day.

- Review current projects. If there are items you won't finish before you depart and can't take with you, put these on your

Master "To Do" List. You'll want to be sure to attend to them when you get home.

- Unless you have the type of job where you are in and out of the office and traveling constantly, you'll want some time to sift through your paperwork prior to the trip. (No matter how organized you are for your trip, there is a strong likelihood that your in box still has pressing items in it.) Come in 30 to 60 minutes early the day before your departure. You'll never get uninterrupted time late in the day. One more time, go through and review the files that are going with you, adding anything that seems necessary. As you go through the day, you may find additional items to add, but you'll be well organized.

MANAGING THE ONE-PERSON BUSINESS

- Record a voice mail message that indicates that you're away. If you can, provide information on another way to contact you— cell phone, beeper, hotel phone number, etc.
- Check phone messages regularly.

• Ask a friend or family member to check through your mail and send it to you by express delivery. Leave preaddressed envelopes for them to use.

KEEP IT SIMPLE

1. Plan ahead on what work to take with you. You'll want all papers related to the reason you're traveling, but also take along any projects you need to work on while away.

2. Record a new voice mail message that lets people know you're away from the office, and have an automatic e-mail message ready to respond to any e-mails you receive. Your clients and business associates will manage their needs differently if they know you won't be able to get back to them right away.

3. Communicate with your staff what their responsibilities are while you're away. Keep a list of work you've delegated so that you can follow up when you check in or upon your return.

2
TIME MANAGEMENT

WHAT'S AHEAD

An advertising executive returns to her office after traveling to the East Coast to do a presentation; when she gets back to her office, she discovers she's missing one of her carousels of slides.

A sales manager has had a productive business trip that would have been more productive if he hadn't run out of business cards.

A computer consultant fidgets throughout almost every plane trip. He jumps from activity to activity (reading, watching the movie, getting out his laptop, flipping through a magazine), and never really focuses on what he needs to do to better manage his time.

A buyer for children's clothing returns from each business trip feeling totally frazzled. Her briefcase is a mess, and for every day she's gone she spends a day catching up.

Traveling is an unsettling process for the disorganized. To survive and thrive in a job where your work must be portable, you need to focus on setting up systems to make this way of life as uneventful as possible. Those who do so find they can travel without too much stress and may even have a good time in the process.

Here are some helpful ways to manage your time while away so that you don't have to return home and spend time catching up.

KEEPING TRACK OF YOUR LIFE

- Travel with a comprehensive calendar (electronic or paper) that reflects your business appointments as well as the whereabouts of family members while you're gone. By keeping track of family commitments on the same calendar as your business appointments, you'll be able to maintain a closeness because you're on top of what's going on: If you know your son has a softball game at 5 P.M. Friday and you find you can catch an earlier flight, you can call to let him know you're on the way home and should be able to make it before game time. What's more, you won't hurt anyone's feelings by forgetting what is happening in their lives. Nothing disappoints family members more than to have the "away" parent call, having forgotten all about the school concert or the championship game. If the date is on your calendar, then the first words out of your mouth when you call can be: "How was the game?" or "Did the concert go well?" Then they know you care and are thinking of them.

- Keep a Master "To Do" List that goes with you at all times. Note *everything* you need to do or need to check on. This ongoing list serves two helpful purposes:

  1. By getting in the habit of writing down all you have to do, you never forget about anything.

  2. This Master List provides the basis from which to build your daily "to do" items.

      I like using a separate notebook for my list, but you could also use a section of your datebook or your handheld computer.

- When you call in for telephone messages, note them on your Master List, your datebook, or enter them into your handheld computer. When you get back to the office you'll have a complete list of the people whom you need to call.

- Use your Master List, your datebook, or handheld computer to keep track of ideas you get while away, books to read, great quotes, movies to see, errands to do.

- Set up a tickler or "reminder" file system. If you travel frequently, it is all the more important that you set up a system to keep track of the minor details of life, ranging from sending birthday cards to keeping track of dry cleaning tickets. Purchase a box of new file folders:

  — Twelve folders should be labeled with the months.

  — Thirty-one of the new folders should be numbered 1 through 31 for each day of the month.

  — The monthly folders should hold general reminders of tasks to be taken care of that month; the daily folders should hold the specific documents you need. Directions to a conference should be filed on the day you'll need them; the birthday card for your good friend should be filed on the day on which you should mail the card; a reminder to take back library books should be in the folder for the day the books are due.

Before I leave town, I take care of everything due before my return. No more late payments, missed birthdays, or overdue library books.

THE GOOD TIME MANAGER ALWAYS HAS ALONG . . .

- An "on the go" reading file consisting of full magazines—or preferably, articles torn out to lessen the bulk—business correspondence, reports, and industry publications.
- A laptop computer. While short trips may not merit lugging it along every time, having your laptop with you will mean you can stay current with e-mail, and you can get some work done when you have time.
- Ample business cards. If you're out doing business, you need to let people know who you are and how to reach you. If you're at a huge conference and give out your last card, have your office send them to you by next-day delivery.
- A good novel. Sometimes the best way to get through travel delays or a restless night in a hotel is by escaping into someone else's world. If you've got a novel with you, you can do that.

THE GOOD TIME MANAGER ALWAYS . . .

- Allows extra time. Flights are delayed, traffic is snarled, people run late, life happens:
  - Travel the night before if you're worried about making an early morning meeting.
  - Overestimate how long you think it will take to get from meeting to meeting. The time it takes a native to drive across town will be different from the time it may take you.
  - Pad your appointments with extra time. If one client is running late or wants you to stay longer, you won't be nervously looking at your watch. If you arrive early and have extra time, you can get some work done, make phone calls, or read until it's time for your appointment.
- Anticipates problems before they happen, not after. Confirm your plans (or have a staff member do it), from touching bases with the out-of-town clients to double-checking the airlines.

Meetings and Presentations

- Write a checklist of every item used for your presentation. This will make it easy to pack each time you leave town, and it will provide you with a checklist when it's time to pack up again.

- Call ahead to check what will be available to you at your destination. Whether you need an easel, a projector, or electrical tape, see if they can provide what you need. If not, be sure to make a list as to what you must bring along.

- If you can have Internet access from the conference room in which you are presenting, create a special URL address and put your presentation on the Web.

- Be sure you know how all your presentation equipment works before you leave home. Make notes if you need to and arrange to have a technical services person or backup expert on call who can talk you through any problems.

- Have presentation boards made in manageable pieces so you don't have to carry the huge presentation cases.

- If you're carrying videocassettes, never let them go through the airport metal detectors.

- Carry a printout of your slides with you on the plane, not packed. You can review it as you travel.

- See if you can get into the meeting room early (the night before for a breakfast meeting) to set up. If there are problems, you still have time to get help.

- If you're responsible for a display at a trade show, then packing up your clothing is the least of your worries. You have an entire booth to take care of, a process that can take several hours to set up and another couple of hours to dismantle. Here's how to do it as easily as possible:

  — Pack the booth up as you take it down. That way the last section to go into the case is the first one you need to set it up again, and everything is packed in the order in which you'll need it.

  — Pack toolbox, lights, electrical cord, and duct and packing tapes last.

- Carry a file with several preaddressed overnight delivery service slips. When your presentation is over, ship your materials home.

FLIGHT TIME

People have all sorts of opinions as to what the best use of plane time is. Some vary their routine depending on whether they are inbound or outbound, some have established routines they follow no matter what.

First a warning: *Never go through confidential material on the plane. The person sitting beside you or behind you may be a competitor or married to someone who works for a competitor.* Otherwise, here are some suggestions business travelers give:

- Many people review what they need to for their upcoming meetings while outbound; when coming home, it's time to pull out a good book.

- Some travel with note cards, envelopes, and stamps. "I do quick follow-up notes on the plane to those people I've just seen," says one businessman. "That way I've cleared my slate so that when I arrive home, I can focus on what needs to be done there."

- Many business travelers use their trip home to fill out their expense reports. If you've collected all your receipts in an envelope as you've traveled, you can fill out all the paperwork before you get home. If you delay, procrastination will set in and the chance of misplacing the receipts will cause you to take even more time than necessary.

- Pay bills.

- One businesswoman uses flight time to enter all her new contacts into a computer program so that she has easy access to everyone who was in her address book.

- Learn something new. Take along a book, a kit, an audiocassette (there are first-rate college lectures sold on tape now), the instructional method makes no difference, just use the time as a way to expose yourself to something you would never have time for if you were at home.

- One businesswoman loves to do needlework and uses flight time to pursue a hobby she wouldn't normally have time to pursue.

- Write personal letters. Bring along preaddressed, stamped envelopes and letter-writing materials. Estimate the number of letters you think you might have time to write, and bring along enough envelopes for the number of letters. By estimating "write two letters," and getting those written, you'll feel accomplished rather than frustrated that you didn't write five.

- One traveler adds to a journal during flight time: "I note down all the nice things people have done for me along the way, and then when flights are delayed or cabbies are rude, I think back to all the other people who have helped me out."

- Some people like having a Walkman with them. When they want to, they can control their environment and listen to relaxing music.

- Inflight movies are taking on a whole new look now that some airlines are making DVDs available. If you're not flying a plane where this is offered, you can now rent digital movies and a DVD player at many of the larger airports. Either return the unit and the movie to a kiosk at the next airport, or keep it with you and return it at the point of origin.

Keeping Current

- Pick up a local newspaper, or scan the one that is delivered to your hotel room. Catching up on local news will help you relate better to your clients, because you'll have a better understanding of the community where they live.

- Follow your favorite newspaper on the Web. You may need a password to access the Web site from the road, but all those travelers who thrive on reading the newspaper to which they are accustomed can now be satisfied.

- If you're not traveling with your laptop, a new company is distributing paper copies of major national and international newspapers to some major hotels. You can get anything from the *Atlanta Constitution*, the *Manchester Guardian*, or Germany's *Der Tagesspiegel* delivered directly to your room if your hotel participates in the program. Check with the concierge to find out if newspaper availability at the hotel goes beyond the usual range of offerings (the local paper as well as nationals such as *USA Today* and *The Wall Street Journal*).

While Away

- If your cell phone has a range limit, rent one that will operate in the city you're visiting. Ask the concierge to help you locate one, or stop in at the office services area of the hotel.

- Price out transportation. If you are traveling around town by taxi and have several stops to make, call ahead and ask about hiring a car and driver. It will definitely be more convenient, and it may not be that much more expensive than numerous cabs.

- Overwhelmed putting together kits, trying to print out presentation materials, handling phone calls? Hire a local temp to help you with out-of-town details.

- If you work with a client's staff or people whom you hire while away, think of something special to do for them—buy lunch or send flowers. You'll be warmly welcomed on any return visit.

- If you're between appointments, set up an "office" in a hotel lobby. Your briefcase, your laptop, and your cell phone should put you in business for ten minutes or three hours, whatever time you have to fill.

- Tackle a project where you need a good-size block of time in order to accomplish your goal. Says one traveler: "A free evening in a hotel room often gives me a three- or four-hour time block to work on a major project. Not many people think of phoning me while I'm away, so there are few interruptions. If I can accomplish a major task, it really helps free my work and family time when I return home."

- Try to get work-related memos, letters, and thank-you notes written before you return. Do it at night in the hotel room or on the plane coming home.

When You Return

- Go in early to have some concentrated time in the office to catch up.

- Sort and delegate as much of the mail as possible.
- Set a "phone back" period so that all your phoning is done in one block of time.
- Follow up on items you've delegated to others.
- Review your Master "To Do" List, adding to it any leftover items from your trip.

KEEP IT SIMPLE

1. Stay on top of everything you need to do by keeping a Master "To Do" List. This is an ongoing list of everything that you need to do, to check on, or even just to think about. That way good ideas and necessary tasks aren't forgotten.

2. Always allow extra time for everything when you travel. Clients run late, traffic can be bad, everything takes longer than what someone has told you . . . by giving yourself extra time, you will rarely have to panic about missing a plane or being late for an important business appointment.

3. Take control of any pockets of free time that occur while you're away. If you have a free moment while traveling, carefully consider what you want to do. On a plane, the answer may range from "nap" to "work," or if you happen into an entire free afternoon in a new city, you have almost unlimited possibilities. Choose well.

3

MANAGING THE HOMEFRONT:

SECURITY, MAIL, PETS

WHAT'S AHEAD

Household Security
Emergency Numbers
Your Household Notebook

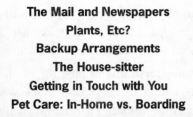

The Mail and Newspapers
Plants, Etc?
Backup Arrangements
The House-sitter
Getting in Touch with You
Pet Care: In-Home vs. Boarding

Whether you take two or twenty-two business trips a year, you can take several steps to safeguard your home and streamline your departures so that the effort in getting away doesn't leave you frazzled and feeling certain you forgot to do something.

Each of the systems recommended in this chapter require time in the initial arrangement; after that, your "while I'm away" plans should be something you can implement with only a phone call or two.

HOUSEHOLD SECURITY

Household security is important whether you travel or not. If you've never had a security expert come through your home or apartment, this is a good time to do so. If you're considering putting in an alarm system, then the alarm company will also recommend lock styles and placement. Their first preference is that your home is secure enough that the alarm will never sound.

If you need additional advice or don't intend to put in an alarm system, get a recommendation from a locksmith. They, too, will be happy to advise you on additional security measures you might take.

- Security companies recommend posting an alarm company sign on your property and affixing stickers to a few ground-level windows. Someone contemplating a break-in will go on to another home if he feels yours is wired with an alarm.

- Purchase timers for your lights, and consider putting a radio on a timer as well. Unless a person studies your home over a long period of time, he or she will be deterred by the sense that someone may be at home some of the time. As more and more homes are wired to be "smart homes," it will be possible to set computer systems so that lights, television, and radio all come on at varying times of day, more convincingly creating the illusion that someone is at home.

- Don't hide a key outside your home. You may think you have the "perfect" hiding place, but professionals are familiar with the fake rocks sold for hiding keys, and they can quickly check under mats and behind mailboxes—all the logical hiding places people think of.

- Select an emergency contact, and plan to leave a key with him or her:

  — If you live in an apartment, the logical choice would be the building's superintendent.

— If you have a house, then select someone who is around home enough so that you could locate the person in an emergency. If nearby neighbors are gone a great deal, then ask a friend. If possible, select someone who comes by your house regularly. That way if newspapers are piling up on the front porch, your contact will notice and do something about it.

— Don't put your name or address on the key you leave with your emergency contact. Instead write on the label a logical (to you and the friend) key word, perhaps the name of your pet. If the keys are stolen from your neighbor's home, the burglar has not obtained easy access to your household as well.

- Keep some of your shades and blinds up as if you were home.
- Leave a simple message on your answering machine, and set it to answer on the first or second ring. A phone that rings and rings is a tip-off to the caller and anyone on or near your property that no one is home.

EMERGENCY NUMBERS

Every household should have a list of emergency numbers posted by each telephone in the home. Even if you live alone, you may get flustered if a fire should break out. If Aunt Bessie is staying with you, you need to provide her with the information she would need if an emergency were to occur while you were out.

- Put your street address on this list. In an emergency the information you know best can fly out of your mind.

- Here is what belongs on your list:

Your Address _____

Your Home Phone Number _____

Your Work Number _____

Cell Phone Number and Beeper _____

Emergency: 9-1-1

Fire _____

Police _____

Poison Control Center _____

Ambulance _____

Electric Company Emergency Number _____

Gas Company Emergency Number _____

Doctor and Address _____

_____

Pharmacy _____

Neighbor Who Would Help _____

In-town Relative to Notify _____

Taxi _____

Nearest Hospital and Address _____

_____

And if there are children or pets:

Pediatrician (Phone Number and Address) _____

_____

Pediatric Dentist _____

Each Child's Name, Birth Date, and Blood Type:

_____

_____

_____

Regular Veterinarian _____

24-Hour Animal Hospital _____

YOUR HOUSEHOLD NOTEBOOK

Whether you are leaving an empty home or leaving children at home with a spouse or a sitter, everyone needs to create a "what to do if . . ." notebook that includes several types of information. The person in charge of your household should know the basics of how your household works (where the main water valve is, where the circuit breaker unit is located, etc.) in case of an emergency.

- Purchase a brightly colored looseleaf notebook (a bright color is easier to identify in the frantic moments of an emergency), looseleaf paper, and pocket dividers.

- The first page of your notebook should be a photocopy of the sheet of emergency numbers that are posted by your telephones.

- These additional numbers should be listed in your notebook:

Electrician _____

Heating and A/C Repair _____

Plumber _____

Repair People for

Kitchen Appliances _____

Washer/Dryer _____

Handyman _____

Any additional numbers that might be helpful

_____

_____

- The next section of your notebook should provide information (possibly including diagrams) that explains how to turn off the household water, electricity, and gas.

- The household notebook should be kept in your kitchen for use by you or anyone who might be staying in your home in your absence.

- If a friend or neighbor watches your home when you are away, invite him over for a tour of the house. Give him/her a photocopy of the pages from the emergency notebook along with any additional emergency telephone numbers he/she should have, show him/her where all emergency shut-off valves are, and provide a demonstration of the alarm system if you have one. (Most alarm systems have a special code that can be given to nonfamily members, and the alarm can be set to accept that code at specific times, such as when you are away.) If your neighbor agrees to cover for you regularly, offer to return the favor.

THE MAIL AND NEWSPAPERS

Making plans as to what to do about the mail and newspapers has as much to do with security as it does with convenience. A pile of newspapers on the lawn or a box delivered to your front porch that remains there for a few days is a sure sign that no one is home. The best system for managing both the newspapers and the mail is to ask a friend to look after things for you, or hire a neighborhood teen to do so. Here are some other suggestions:

- You may want to cancel the newspaper if you're gone for more than a day or two.

- If you live in a neighborhood with a friendly package delivery person or postal worker, you may be able to ask them to leave packages or bulky mail on an out-of-view porch or in a protected alcove of your home.

- For lengthy trips, it may be worth it to have mail held at the post office. This eliminates anyone having to take care of it while you're away. The drawback is that you have to arrange to get to the post office to pick it up after your return, delaying the time when you can start processing it.

- In homes, door slots for mail have an advantage over mailboxes: several days' worth of mail can be dropped through the slot and no one needs to tend it for you. Mailboxes, of course, need to be emptied by someone.

PLANTS, ETC?

If you live alone and travel a great deal, give careful thought to the acquisition of both pets and houseplants. While both can be wonderful additions to any home, they may add a level of complication to your life that you don't need.

If you have a friendly neighbor who is happy to help with either animals or plants, or both, then this may not be an issue for you, but if you relish being free to travel, then why burden yourself with responsibilities that aren't necessary right now?

BACKUP ARRANGEMENTS

Even if you have cancelled the newspapers and you know that your mail will be slipped through the door slot, you still need another pair of eyes watching the house. The regular delivery person may be on vacation and the replacement person may accidentally keep delivering your paper, or a bulky package may have been slipped halfway into the screen door. Regardless of what arrangements you've made, have a backup plan in place in case something goes wrong.

THE HOUSE-SITTER

Even without children or pets, some people are more comfortable having someone stay in their home while they are away. The longer the trip, the more appeal this solution has.

Your first choice, of course, would be a family member or friend whom you know. Perhaps your lengthy business trip to the Far East can be a time when your nephew stays in your New York City apartment and takes advantage of the city's many attractions, or perhaps your cousin would like to write a novel and your suburban home will offer her the peace and quiet she desires.

If no logical person presents herself, then ask around. College students who baby-sit or people who pet-sit would all be excellent candidates. Ask for and check references.

Once hired:

- Ask the person to stop by so the two of you can meet. Show her or him around the house, pointing out the bedroom to be used, and demonstrating how the appliances work.

- Show the house-sitter the emergency notebook, and take her/him to the basement to show her/him the turn-off valves and switches described in the notebook.

- Provide a note that indicates garbage and recycling days as well as specifics about any pickups and deliveries, when the lawn is cut, and when cleaning help arrives and how they get into the home. These things may seem routine to you, but they would not be to anyone else.

- Specify guidelines for use of the house. If a college student will be living in your home for a week or two, it might be unrealistic to say guests are never allowed. However, you may want to specify no parties or entertaining more than one person at a time.

Getting in Touch with You

Whether it's an emergency, a question, or just a concern, the person who is responsible for looking after your home in your absence should have all applicable telephone numbers for the time you're away.

Pet Care: In-Home vs. Boarding

A pet-sitter who comes to stay in your home with your pet is certainly the most pet-centered form of care. For many people, however, this is more expensive, requires more arranging, and is more invasive than other alternatives for their pet. Before thinking you have to hire an in-home replacement for yourself while you're away, consider locating a well-regarded person who will board your pet. Some people will take a limited number of animals in to live as household pets for a few days. (Groomers often do this or know people who do.) In addition, today there are lovely boarding kennels that are designed to be canine- or feline-style hotels, complete with pet beds and television (tuned to the Animal Planet channel, I trust).

A good, "normal" kennel will also be just fine. Be sure it is recommended by people whom you trust, and so long as your pet is happy to arrive each time, you know the animal is in safe hands.

When screening a place for your pet to stay, ask the following questions:

- How long are they in their crates?
- How often do the animals go out?
- Do they socialize with other animals? (This could be a positive if your dog likes to play; this may make you nervous if your dog is timid or very old.)
- Can the boarding place accommodate special diets?
- Ask for references.

If it's the type of place where you can drop in without phoning ahead, do so. It will give you an opportunity to observe the true level of hygiene and the care the pets receive.

If you have an unusual pet or an animal with special needs (requires frequent medication, etc.), you may need to ask a friend or family member to help, or consider the pet-sitter option.

Anyone with whom you leave your pet should be left with emergency information.

EMERGENCY INFO FOR SPOT

Spot: Spot is eight years old; weighs about 21 lbs.
Owners: Mary and John Smith 203-555-3331
          6 Oak Lane
          New Canaan, CT 06840
Vet: Dr. Miller 203-555-1756
In case of emergency, nearest person to contact:
Neighbor: Susan Williams 203-555-3440
          We can be reached at 1-800-555-4915
          or leave message: 212-555-8635 (John's cell phone)
          or 1-800-555-2337 (beeper)
(I'll pick up the dog Wednesday night, April 19.)

KEEP IT SIMPLE

1. Have your home evaluated by a security expert, and do what is necessary to make it safe.

2. Prepare a "what to do if . . ." household notebook that can be left for anyone watching your home.

3. Always provide your telephone number to anyone who is responsible for your children, your home, or your pets while you're away.

4
LEAVING KIDS AT HOME

WHAT'S AHEAD

Creating a List of Vital Information
Household Lists and Schedules
Details for Baby
Household Organization
If the Stay Is at Grandma's or Aunt Nell's
Advance Prep
For the Occasional Traveler
In Touch from Afar
On Your Return
Mixing Family and Business?

ny businessperson who is fortunate enough to have a take-charge spouse or a loyal caregiver who is capable of taking care of the home and children while he or she is away should be eternally grateful. To leave on a business trip without having to arrange for mail delivery, package pickups, household security, or the 1,001 different arrangements that are necessary if you are leaving children at home is a gift beyond compare.

CREATING A LIST OF VITAL INFORMATION

- Whether your children are left with your spouse, a nanny, or a nearby aunt, the adult in charge should have emergency information. Purchase a one-inch looseleaf notebook and place the following important information in it; if your children are going to Grandma's for one of the nights you're gone, the notebook can go along with them. Include:

  — Medical history of each child, including any allergies or dietary restrictions. If the child takes medication regularly, instructions should be recorded here.

  — List of important telephone numbers, as described in the previous chapter. One list of emergency numbers should be posted by each phone in the household; a copy should go in this notebook as well. You may want to add a few more numbers that might be helpful during this particular trip, such as the number of the softball team coach or the number of the school attendance office in the event she isn't feeling well.

— Medical insurance information.

— Consent form authorizing another adult to make emergency medical care decisions for your child in your absence. (The proper wording can vary from state to state, so check with your doctor for correct wording.)

— Your itinerary, complete with flight information and a detailed day-to-day schedule of where you'll be. Include phone numbers and dates and times as well as the time zone.

ITINERARY

My Cell Phone Number: 973–555–2211
Pager: 1–888–985–5423
The Fletcher Hotel: 1–800–555–1234
Eastern Standard Time

HOUSEHOLD LISTS AND SCHEDULES

- A daily list that includes each child's schedule as well as all household tasks to be completed each day is vital to the success of those—your sitter or your spouse, or the two of them together—you leave in charge of the household in your absence.

- If you have a regular caregiver, then she will know the basics. The list you provide should cover the times of the day when she's not usually there or the tasks you normally do that she'll need to absorb.

- If you use an oversize kitchen calendar that lists all the children's activities, use gummy-backed notes for any additional information. Attach the notes to the appropriate part of the calendar, and your family can remove it as the various tasks are completed.

- For a new caregiver, a visiting grandmother, or anyone hired to cover for you for a single trip, you'll need to create two lists. Samples of both are included.

  1. The basics of managing the household (see sample). This list should be one you can reuse for other trips.

  2. A daily list of activities. This list provides your children's schedules, including specifics about meals, homework, after-school activities, and playdates.

- Create the lists so that you have a day or two to double-check them as you go through your routine. Be sure to review them carefully with your caregiver or spouse before you leave.

Household Management List

Monday

— 6:45 A.M., walk dog and put out food and fresh bowl of water.

— Clean up kitchen and bathroom.

— Return videos borrowed over the weekend.

— Go grocery shopping.

— 6 P.M., feed dog: one bowl dry food; change water.

— Prepare school lunches after dinner.

— Run dishwasher.

— Empty dishwasher; lay out breakfast dishes.

Tuesday

— 6:45 A.M., walk dog, put out food and fresh bowl of water.

— Straighten kitchen, bathroom.

— Start laundry; fold and put away.

— Pick up dry cleaning.

— 6 P.M., feed dog: one bowl of dry food, change water.

— Run dishwasher.

— Empty dishwasher; lay out breakfast dishes.

CHILDREN'S SCHEDULE

Monday, September 8

7:15 A.M., wake Helen (dresses self).

7:30, wake David—help him get dressed.

7:45, breakfast (Helen: orange juice, cereal and muffin; David: milk, cereal and apple slices.)

8:15, walk Helen to bottom of hill and wait for school bus. Bus arrives between 8:20–25 A.M. (She should have her backpack and lunch; fleece sweatshirt if it's chilly.)

8:45, drive David to nursery school.

12:00, nursery school pickup. Jason comes for playdate. (Mother: Sue Smith, 555–2211.) She'll pick up about 2:30. Give the boys peanut butter and jelly sandwiches and orange sections for lunch.

3:15, meet Helen's bus at bottom of hill; bus arrives 3:15–25 P.M.

4:00–4:30, Helen should start homework and may need help from you during this time. Homework can take from 30–60 minutes. Remind her to put finished work in her backpack.

6:00, dinner. Pasta with sauce.

7:00, bathtime. Helen washes her hair every other night.

7:30, help children lay out clothes for the next day.

8:00, David goes to bed. (Brush teeth.) He gets two stories and sleeps with his special quilt. If you can't find it, check the family room. He often takes it there when he watches television.

8:30, bedtime for Helen; she reads for another 20 minutes.

DETAILS FOR BABY

Both you and your baby will be happier if your spouse or caregiver maintains the baby's schedule while you are away. Providing accurate information is key, so all feedings and the amounts given should be written down. A complete schedule for the morning might include the following.

BABY'S MORNING SCHEDULE

7:00, baby wakes; change diaper.
7:30, breakfast:
3 T mashed bananas
3 T rice cereal
7 oz. formula.
8:00, 1 dropper baby vitamins.
9:00, morning walk (don't forget sunblock and hat).
10:00–11:30, nap.
12:00, lunch:
3 T strained vegetables (peas or sweet potatoes)
3 T fruit (applesauce or pear)
7 oz. formula.

HOUSEHOLD ORGANIZATION

- Cook ahead. Even male travelers can ease some of the burden of their being away by helping out with meal planning and prep on a weekend. That makes one less thing for the at-home spouse or caregiver to have to worry about during the trip.

- If you are the parent who handles morning preparations with younger children, consider doing some of it in advance: Provide a Ziploc plastic bag for each day you'll be gone, and put into it either outfits for each day or something your child needs for school. If "share" is on Fridays, then help your child choose an item in advance and pack it in the bag. The at-home spouse or caregiver will appreciate having one less thing to remember to do!

- Routine is the secret to a peaceful household while you are away. Try not to change sitters right before a trip, and while it's nice to let the sitter offer a few special privileges, the children are better off staying with their normal schedule and knowing what the limits are.

- Explain to the children relevant instructions that you've left with the sitter: "I've told Susan you can stay up an extra half hour on Saturday night, but otherwise, I expect you to follow family rules."

- School-age children should participate in household chores (fixing their lunches, helping in the kitchen) when you are in town as well as when you are away. Giving them responsibilities will also streamline life while you're gone. If eleven-year-old Billy makes his own lunch, then the caregiver needn't be told to do so. (Your "to do" list for the caregiver may need to ask that she remind Billy to do so, however.)

- Plan normal activities. Arrange playdates with favorite friends, and if you have a nearby relative, ask her to invite them to go out to dinner one night.

- Carpool changes should be written down and pointed out to both your caregiver and your child.

- If your trip conflicts with a special event (school play, championship softball game), see if the trip can be rescheduled. If it can't, try to find a way to make up for missing it. Ask to attend a dress rehearsal of a recital or play, and see if someone might videotape significant portions of the softball game championship.

- Ask a neighbor or a nearby relative to check in with your caregiver while you're away. An unannounced visit to drop off fresh strawberries or some other offering will permit her to give you helpful feedback on how things are going while you're away.

- If you're gone for more than a few days, consider hiring a baby-sitter to relieve your baby-sitter, unpaid relative, or your spouse. Providing them with a break and a support system can make it a more pleasant time for kids and caregiver alike.

IF THE STAY IS AT GRANDMA'S OR AUNT NELL'S

Sometimes it is easier for the caregiver, and fun for the children, if they stay at the caregiver's home while you are away. During a summer business trip, you might drop them at a distant grandparent's home—a treat for all involved. If your children will stay somewhere other than home while you're gone, here's what you need to do:

- Just as you would if they were staying in your home, give the relative or caregiver with whom you're leaving the children your notebook with relevant emergency information. If your child is staying in a distant community, then the caregiver can rely on her own network, but having the name of the children's pediatrician for a quick phone consultation may still be helpful. Be sure that a signed copy of the emergency consent form is included.

- Also include general information such as nap schedules and bedtimes. While you can't dictate how the other household should run during your children's stay, everyone will welcome having some guidelines to follow that will help make your children's stay more manageable.

- If the location where they are staying is in your own community, provide the caregiver with a list of telephone numbers of friends as well as any carpooling schedules that will be in operation while you're away.

ADVANCE PREP

If you travel regularly, then your children know what to expect, but there are still ways to ease the time when you're away:

- Try to make a policy of not traveling on birthdays and anniversaries. While celebrations can be rescheduled for later in the week or the weekend, the family will always remember the event as "the time when Mom [or Dad] was away."

- Avoid weekend travel when you can. Planning for the children is easier during the week when there is structure. If you must, travel late Sunday to minimize the weekend time away.

- Mark your business trips on the Family Calendar. That way your absence never comes as a surprise.

- Prerecord stories or messages. One family purchased inexpensive tape recorders for each family member. When the mother travels, she records messages for each person for the number of days she'll be gone. The messages range from jokes and reminders to stories she records for the younger children. The tape left for Dad contains reminders of what needs to be taken care of each day.

- For young children, use an ordinary notebook to create a picture book that tells the "story" of your absence. Devote one page for each day you'll be gone, and divide the page into two parts. The top half should show a picture of what your child will be doing (going to nursery school? Playing at Grandma's?); the bottom half should show where you are on that day (sitting in an airplane? Giving a speech?) The "day-I-return" page might show the two of you, or the whole family, doing something fun together.

- Some families leave a sticker or a small piece of candy in a bowl for each day a parent will be gone. The child is allowed to take one item from the collection each day, and this provides a way for young ones to measure time. (A caregiver can also turn this into a great counting exercise.)

- Share your trip with your children by pointing out on a map where you're going and talking a bit about what you expect (or know) it will be like: "San Diego is by the ocean, and the hotel where I'll stay is on the beach. Maybe one day we can go there together." If you travel a great deal to different locations, you can teach your children a lot about geography!

- If you travel regularly, establish a going-away ritual, a special game with a preschooler, or a trip to the bookstore for a school-age child; perhaps a quick dinner out with a teenager.

- If your child is going through a difficult time, see if you can postpone your trip or shorten it a bit. Or consider whether it's appropriate to take your child with you (special "Mom or Dad time" can sometimes work wonders). If these solutions are impossible, then make a date with your child to do something special when you come back home again.

- Make certain there is an up-to-date family photograph in your household. Placing a picture of the two of you by your child's bed is helpful, too.

FOR THE OCCASIONAL TRAVELER

If a parent travels frequently, then the children understand that this is just part of the weekday routine. However, if you travel only occasionally, you bear the additional challenge of helping family members understand that you'll be gone and exactly what that involves.

- Children should be told of your trip in advance. A day or two is plenty of warning for little ones (even a child as young as two deserves being told directly that you are going away). Children seven and older can be told a week or so in advance. Point it out to them on the Family Calendar. Tell them where you're going, why, and when you'll return.

- If the stay is somewhat indefinite (until the production line at a new factory is up and running, for example), overestimate the time you'll be gone.

IN TOUCH FROM AFAR

- Two additions to your telephone system can make it easier to stay in touch with the family:

  — A cell phone. While you almost certainly have one for work-related tasks, you'll find it will also be helpful with family matters. You can call home from a parking lot or a hotel lobby without having to locate a phone, and the children can call you directly and leave messages as they need to. Talking regularly lets you be more a part of their lives even when you're far away.

  — An 800 number. The addition of an 800 number to your home line can make it easy for you to phone from an airport, the hotel lobby, or your hotel room. If you're in an area where cell phone connections are unreliable, this could be the perfect solution for phoning home spontaneously.

- In addition to quick phone calls during the day, set a specific time for a longer chat. This offers your child a time when he or she knows homework can be discussed, or long complaints can be aired. If the regularly scheduled call needs to be in the evening, try to find a time that is before dinner (or just after). If upsetting issues are discussed, you and your children will both sleep better if the calls aren't made right at bedtime.

- Phone at the appointed hours. These calls can be upsetting—young children may cry or even refuse to speak to you, but don't be alarmed so long as the caregiver provides you with a reasonable report. The upset may be a one-time occurrence because of something that happened at school, or your child may simply need to express his feelings with someone with whom he feels safe (you).

- Avoid getting angry or upset with your children on the phone. If they've misbehaved, the issue should either be handled by the at-home parent or the caregiver (with your permission), or dealt with when you get home. Expressing unhappiness with your child should be reserved for times when you can both talk about how you feel and resolve the conflict.

- After listening carefully to your child, share one or two things about your trip so they'll know a bit about what you are doing.

- For children school age and older, e-mail may be a preferable manner of communicating on days when they are busy with lots of activities. E-mail is also ideal when different time zones put you at a dinner meeting about the time the kids are ready to go to bed. And even if you do speak by phone, send them occasional messages, including news about the city you're visiting.

- Don't forget faxes. A difficult homework sheet or a nursery school drawing can be faxed to you so that you can help or admire as needed.

- One dad who is at meetings in the evenings when his small children are going to bed has requested that they be his wake-up call in the morning.

ON YOUR RETURN

- Is a "coming home" gift appropriate? Absolutely. It's something for the kids to look forward to, and if they've been good sports about your being away then they've earned it. The best gifts are inexpensive presents that your child might actually use. Don't bring them a key chain with the Eiffel Tower on it unless they have a collection of key chains. Instead bring your artist a special pen for drawing or your little dancer a book about a ballerina. While the thought of bringing your child something that represents your trip seems tempting, what generally happens to all tourist curios is they become junk that needs to be thrown away. Here's another secret: If you bring thoughtful presents for each child, there is no rule that the gift must actually be purchased on this trip. If you see several possibilities (that can be easily packed) on one trip, stock up and dispense them slowly. This system is a great time-saver.

- Don't hold your family to the highest of standards when you come home. If those at home managed to keep the household running smoothly, they've done their most important job. Nonetheless, you shouldn't have to spend your first day back cleaning. Ask family members to pitch in with specific family tasks that can't wait, and otherwise, catch up with home chores gradually so that family can be your first priority.

- If the day after your return is a business day, try to come home from work a little earlier that day, and be sure that you all have the opportunity to have a meal together as soon as possible. You might want to take everyone out.

- If your spouse or a visiting relative has been in charge while you were away, consider sending them on a "break" as soon as the hellos are said. The at-home person is undoubtedly mentally or physically drained (maybe both!), and a nice walk, sneaking upstairs to the bedroom to read a book, or anything that is not child-related will be very much appreciated right now.

MIXING FAMILY AND BUSINESS?

- Sometimes families actually look forward to business trips, because they get to go along. If you have a trip to an interesting place, consider whether your frequent flyer miles or a reasonable car trip can let your family come and join you for the weekend. It's a wonderful bonus to your business travel, and it provides pleasure for the family when they get to come along.

- Or you may want to take just one: If you or your spouse travel a great deal, consider whether any of your trips might offer an opportunity to take a child along. Little ones can be left with hotel sitters for brief periods of time, and teenagers will enjoy the freedom of lounging around until you're available to do something. Providing that you have substantial pockets of free time, it can provide significant parent-child time together.

- Taking a child on a business trip is an added responsibility, so select a trip when you'll be able to sneak away for lunch or take the afternoon off to be with your child.

- An in-room refrigerator can make it easier to keep milk and cheese so that you're not totally dependent on room service or the hotel cafe.

- Check with the hotel to see what family services are offered. Some hotels now have playgrounds; many have pools; some even offer on-site "day camps" over weekends, during major conferences, and during the summer; most will recommend sitters or a bonded service. If you choose to book a sitter, call the sitter in advance so that you'll have a sense of what to expect when you arrive.

- If you're renting a car, request a car seat, if needed.

- To the extent possible, maintain your child's normal sleeping and eating schedule while you're away.

While taking a child along with you on business can be a fair amount of additional work, you'll remember your business trip to New York much longer if you also got to take your ten-year-old to the Empire State Building.

KEEP IT SIMPLE

1. A spouse or caregiver should be left with emergency information and a schedule of household tasks that need to be taken care of as well as a list of each child's daily activities.

2. Make a point of being in touch frequently. Call at a prearranged time but send e-mail messages and phone at other times when you can.

3. When you arrive home, arrange time to see your family, and send the at-home spouse or caregiver off for a well-deserved few hours of his or her own.

PART TWO

BEING

EQUIPPED

5
THE
EVER-READY
BRIEFCASE

WHAT'S AHEAD

The Right Bag
Double Duty: Briefcase as Pocketbook, Too
The Organized Briefcase
Briefcase "Must-Haves"
Helpful Supplies When You're On the Go
And the Personals . . .
Using Your Briefcase Well
Major Cleanouts

When I board the train for a morning commute into Manhattan, I am amazed by the number of styles of briefcases I see: There are a few men (and in this case it is only men) carrying the traditional hard-sided cases, and after that, almost anything goes: I see back-pack-style briefcases, totes-on-wheels being used as briefcases, and soft cases made of all types of materials. Then there are the styles intended for the beach and those that look like they have been to a war zone—beaten, torn, and "attacked." The cases clip, snap, buckle, zip, hook, and Velcro shut, but invariably there is one constant. All styles seem to come in one color—black.

If you haven't purchased a new case recently, there are many options today. The newer briefcases of today offer advantages unavailable only a few years ago. From the new types of materials to the inner pockets designed to hold the latest electronic devices, the briefcases on the market now are better suited for today's active workstyles. Whether you're driving to a meeting in the next town or taking a night flight to Hong Kong, it's important to have a case that's right for you.

THE RIGHT BAG

To select the best briefcase for you, look for ones with these features:

- **Lightweight.** With today's new materials, you need not carry a heavy briefcase anymore. Look for a soft-sided bag made of lightweight material. "Getting ahead" no longer requires that you sport a standard-issue leather briefcase or a hard-sided suitcase model.

- **"All-weather" materials.** In a storm your papers won't get soaked. Stay away from materials that don't hold up over time, show stains, and don't wipe clean.

- **A model that zips or snaps closed.** The contents of your case will stay dry and secure.

- **Detachable shoulder strap.** While you may not always need it, the extra strap gives you the option of carrying the bag on your shoulder to keep your hands free.

- **Exterior pocket.** Use it for the newspaper, an umbrella, and any other items you want to have easily accessible.

- **Interior pockets (the more the better) for supplies.** You can substitute by using small, zippered pouches (preferably transparent).

DOUBLE DUTY: BRIEFCASE AS POCKETBOOK, TOO

Carrying a purse and a briefcase is a handful, particularly if you need to carry anything else as well. To make your briefcase do double duty, put the most important of your purse items (money, credit cards, toiletries, and tissues) in a small pouch-style purse. Carry it in the briefcase when traveling or going from meeting to meeting; pull it out to carry alone when slipping out of a meeting on a quick errand or for lunch.

THE ORGANIZED BRIEFCASE

- To keep an organized briefcase, you'll want several file folders and a #10 envelope:
  - Your on-the-go papers should all be stored within labeled file folders ("to read," "action," "to file," "work completed," etc).
  - Use a #10 envelope to hold receipts for business expenses. Label it "receipts."

BRIEFCASE "MUST-HAVES"

- Every briefcase should contain these basics:

  — Calendar and address book or personal digital assistant to keep track of your schedule and/or any people whom you need to reach while you're out of the office.

  — Business cards.

  — Pad of paper; even the devoted computer user will find that there are times when a plain old pad of paper is most convenient for making notes.

  — Pens, pencils, highlighter. Always carry more than one pen and pencil. If someone borrows one or you lose one during the day, you'll have a spare.

  — A few computer diskettes.

  — "Pen"-style flashlight for emergencies.

  — Reading material or on-the-go paperwork (all the miscellaneous mail and five-minute work that you didn't have time to finish at the office) for idle moments.

- Put two dollars in quarters in an interior pocket of your briefcase. If you're short on change and want to rent a luggage cart or need to use a pay phone or feed a parking meter, you've got some spare change.

- If you don't have a cell phone or may travel out of range, carry a phone card with you.
- After you've packed these basics, be selective about the other items you need. If the briefcase becomes too heavy, it will increase your fatigue.

HELPFUL SUPPLIES WHEN YOU'RE ON THE GO

- If you travel or are out of the office for the better part of a week, here are other items that will come in handy:
    — Office tools such as scissors, tape dispenser, small stapler, rubber bands, ruler, miniature pencil sharpener.
    — Clip-it tool for cutting out articles.
    — Sticky-backed notepad.
    — Stamps.
    — Calculator.
    — Recorder for taking notes. Some people like the minicassettes, but take a look at the new digital recorders created specifically for on-the-go note-taking. They are small (small enough to be held in the closed palm of your hand) and have "file" and "priority" features (notes can be recorded into different files for playback, and priority can be assigned to cer-

tain messages). Some are so tiny that the buttons may be difficult for a person with large fingers to use; shop for the model that is sized best for you. *Try before you buy*.

- If you primarily travel by car, some of these items could be packed in a separate bag or container and kept in the car.

AND THE PERSONALS . . .

— A few safety pins for fastening a hem or holding a loose button.

— Tissues.

— Moist towelettes.

— Toothbrush/dental floss.

— Extra collar stays and socks for men, or pantyhose for women.

— Medical kit (a few adhesive strips, pain reliever, allergy medicine, antacid tablets).

— A "power bar" or nonperishable snack of some type. "When you're traveling, you can't always control when you eat," explains one woman. "If you're famished, it really helps to have something with you."

If you're checking your suitcase through on a flight, consider any other toiletries or necessities you would need just in case your bag is delayed.

USING YOUR BRIEFCASE WELL

The key to functioning well throughout the day is having with you everything you need without carrying too much.

- As soon as you know you will be attending a particular meeting, establish a file. Everything from the agenda to appropriate client information should be put into it. By the date of the meeting, you'll find that almost everything you need has already been collected.

- If you'll be leaving early in the morning, pack your briefcase the day before.

- Leave a note on top of your case listing any items that need to be packed at the last minute.

- Instead of writing ideas on scraps of paper and dropping them into the bottom of your bag, note them on extra pages of your calendar, enter them into your electronic organizer (PDA), or establish a small notebook in which to keep track of this type of information. When you get back to the office, add these items to your Master List.

- If your briefcase has two distinct compartments, designate a "to do" side and a "done" side. By placing items into your briefcase according to their status, you've already begun the sorting process.
- When you get back to the office, be certain to empty your briefcase of the papers and files, sorting as you go. Items left in the briefcase for more than a day can easily be forgotten.

MAJOR CLEANOUTS

Trips are a perfect time for a major briefcase cleanout:

- Spread out a towel on the floor or on the bed and remove every paper, pen, and highlighter from your briefcase, placing it on the towel.
- Sort as you go. Old pens, bent paper clips, and dried-out highlighters should be tossed.
- Review the papers within your briefcase. Those that you no longer need to carry with you should be tossed or transferred to a pocket of your suitcase with a label as to where to file it when you return to the office.
- Wipe out the dust and paper scraps that may have collected at the bottom of the case and repack.
- Note down any supplies that are missing so that you can restock.

KEEP IT SIMPLE

1. Choose a lightweight, weatherproof bag that zips closed to keep briefcase items dry and secure.
2. Take what you need but no more than you need.
3. Don't dump things into your briefcase during the day. Use file folders for papers and a #10 envelope for business receipts. Notes and telephone numbers should be written in your calendar or recorded into your personal digital assistant. This will save you time when you return to your office.

6

THE CAR:

YOUR MOBILE OFFICE

WHAT'S AHEAD

Setting Up Your Mobile Office
Car Basics
Don't Leave Home Without . . .
On the Road
General Supplies and Paper Management
Work in Progress
Protecting What's Yours
Keeping Track of Mileage

Mobility. That's the watchword for the business world today. You don't need to be in your office to receive a phone call, to pick up e-mail, to access the Web, or even to receive a fax—you can do all those things from your car. As a result, more and more workers are setting up temporary offices, complete with laptops and cell phones, in roadside restaurants when they stop for a bite to eat. Those who patronize restaurants with drive-through windows are converting their cars into workstations and stopping in parking lots to get some "paperwork" done.

And even if your car only sees business use once or twice a month, there are ways to keep all your business materials handy and organized.

Here's how to make your car complement the way you do business.

SETTING UP YOUR MOBILE OFFICE

Papers all over the place, coffee cups rolling around the floor, your briefcase in the trunk, your overcoat in the car . . . How *should* you set up your mobile office?

- Begin by emptying the car of accumulated debris. Dig the gum wrappers out of the ashtrays, look under the seats for the stray shopping receipts, and ask the kids to remove the soccer ball from the backseat. (If your "mobile office" doubles as the family car, purchase a plastic crate, and place it in the trunk to hold sports equipment and other weekend-related items.)

- Toss the old, tattered maps you've had in the glove compartment and start new. Even with what seems to be good written directions, a good map of the area is a necessity. A recent map will show current road construction as well as on- and off-ramp changes. Be sure to select a map that has side roads well marked in case you need to create your own detour.

- Take the car to the car wash and make sure it also gets well vacuumed. You may want to consider getting it "detailed" a couple of times per year. One woman was shamed into it by the owner of a detail shop who said, "Would you ever let your living room carpet look like *that*?" Afterward she said it was a great investment because her car looked like new.

- Now you're prepared to outfit your car with office equipment and supplies. Within your car there are four main sections where office supplies and papers can be easily stored:

  — The visor.

  — The dashboard.

  — The passenger seat.

  — The trunk.

The right organizing products will permit you to use each of these areas of the car efficiently. A good office supplies store may sell some car organizers, but check the Internet. There are Web sites dedicated to selling mobile office products.

- Among the items you'll choose from:

  — Visor organizers: holds glasses, maps, directions, pens, and highlighter.

  — Cell phone holders that attach to the windshield or dashboard with suction cups. Also on the market are adapters that can temporarily transform your regular hand-held cell phone into a hands-free phone for use in the car.

  — Automobile desks and notebook platforms. Some buckle into the passenger seat, others have a pedestal base. Most have a nonskid surface where you can place a laptop computer without risk of it sliding around while you drive. Some swivel out of the way while driving and can be turned back closer to you when you are parked and need to work. Most have storage bins, some large enough to hold portable printers. Those that detach from the car easily also come with carrying cases, making it easy to take the desk with you to use in your hotel room on an overnight stay.

  — Steering wheel notebook holder. For those who don't need anything as elaborate as an in-car desk, there are notebook platforms that can be attached to the steering wheel for use when you are parked.

- — Trunk organizers. These range from file boxes and crates to a trunk-lid organizer that provides space for books and notebooks.

- And while you're organizing, don't forget the standbys:

  - — A backseat organizer with pockets will absorb glove compartment overflow or offer a better system for you than getting in and out of your trunk regularly. Use it to store anything from maps to an emergency flashlight.

  - — A CD or tape organizer. You'll want to control what you listen to, so be sure to have a way to hold it all.

- If you're on the road a lot, consider an in-car fax. You can purchase a machine that attaches to your cellular or portable telephone with a special jack. The machine runs on battery power or can be plugged into your cigarette lighter.

CAR BASICS

- Be sure to have important car documents (registration, insurance card) with you. Place these papers in a protective envelope and store in the glove compartment.

- Join an automobile club. In addition to the Automobile Association of America (AAA), there are new Internet motor club companies that also offer benefits, including rescuing you if you have a breakdown. Membership services now range from mapping routes and offering hotel discounts to providing the location of the best coffee shop or quick printer near where you are staying.

- Take good care of your car. Establish a regular maintenance schedule to reduce the likelihood of being waylaid by a breakdown.

- Every car should be equipped for emergencies: A flashlight, a lighted magnifier for night map-reading, a first aid kit, flares, a tire jack, tools, some kitty litter (for icy conditions), de-icing spray, an empty gas can, some bottled water, and a blanket should all be stored in a canvas bag in the trunk.

- Make certain you have a properly inflated spare tire. Having a flat is bad enough, but not having a replacement if you need it would be quite distressing.

- Keep a spare key for your car in your wallet so that you're never caught without a key.

- More and more cars are now being created with global positioning satellite access that provides verbal directions to your destination, meaning that one day map-reading may be unnecessary. Nonetheless, keep some maps in the car. Like all computers, these can go down at times, in which case you'll need paper substitutes for finding your way around.

- Always start out with some accessible snacks, bottled water, and anything you'd like to munch on. This will eliminate stops you need to make "because you're starved," and by taking along healthier food you enjoy, you delay the time when you almost inevitably have to compromise by simply eating what is available.

DON'T LEAVE HOME WITHOUT . . .

- An accessible notepad and pen or a pocket-size digital recorder designed for note taking.
- Spare change for parking, and money or a "pass" for getting through tolls (some states now have a computer billing system where cards displaying an electronic "pass" don't need to stop to pay the toll. This is highly convenient for drivers and a real time-saver).
- A supply of paper towels for spills or those unavoidable meals in the car.
- A box of tissues.
- A box of moist wipes.
- A car wastebasket or plastic bags that can be thrown out.
- A folding umbrella.
- A window scraper in winter; a window cover in summer.

ON THE ROAD

On long trips or in extreme weather, keep a careful eye on your car gauges. When you stop:
— Check the oil level.
— Clean the windshield, side and rear windows, outside mirrors, and headlamps.
— Check your windshield wiper fluid level.
— Check tires.
— Take a look under the hood for leaks or loose parts.

GENERAL SUPPLIES AND PAPER MANAGEMENT

- If your business travel is primarily by car, lighten your briefcase load by storing some of the supplies in the car rather than in your briefcase (see Chapter 5). A stapler, scissors, extra adhesive-backed notes, and a box of pens are handy to have along, but you don't need to have them in your briefcase if you have them in the car.

- Purchase a plastic portable file box that closes easily and will fit in the back of your car. Papers won't slip out, and odds and ends won't fall in.

- Within your file box, place several file folders for holding papers.
  — Keep writing paper and envelopes for on-the-road letters.
  — Take along a folder labeled "to file," and "to do on return." The other folders should hold what is appropriate for your business.
  — Carry all sales literature and forms that you normally need. It's much easier to run out to your car file box to get an extra form or brochure for a client than to have to mail it to them after you return to the office.
  — Put a file in the box and use it to hold odds and ends you didn't have time to take care of at the office—magazine subscriptions, memos you didn't have time to read, etc. If you arrive at an appointment early or decide to pull over to rest for fifteen minutes, these are effortless items you can tend to.

WORK IN PROGRESS

Safety must always come first while traveling on business, but there are ways to use your time well.

- Control what you listen to. Whether you select a learning tape, a recording of a lecture you couldn't attend, or an audio book, make good use of the fact that this time is available to you to use.
- Have next to you a minicassette or small dictaphone for recording notes about your latest brainstorm, thoughts for an upcoming

speech, your strategy for the meeting you're to attend later that day, or what you want to do based on any telephone conversation. Trying to write notes about a conversation while driving is difficult to do and can be dangerous.

- You might also consider the latest in technology—-speech recognition digital recorders that let you dictate notes that are quickly converted to editable text once you're back at your PC.

- If you need to make a call, pull over (or get off at the next exit if you're on the highway) and make the call while the car is stopped, or invest in a car phone system with voice-activated dialing and a speakerphone. While statistically, speakerphones do not substantially reduce your risk of having an accident, it is a better option than holding on to a receiver while you drive.

PROTECTING WHAT'S YOURS

- Equipment should be stored out of sight. Locking it in a car trunk is ideal. If you drive a minivan or a sports utility vehicle without a trunk, keep a blanket in the car to throw over anything that might be easily visible.

- Check the appropriate insurance policy to see about coverage. If your equipment belongs to an employer, then talk to personnel about coverage; if it is yours then items that are attached to the car will be covered by a car insurance policy; items that are not attached (fax machine, portable phone) must be covered under your homeowner's policy.

KEEPING TRACK OF MILEAGE

Careful record keeping is very important if you plan to claim mileage on your income tax return. You can:

- Record mileage in your palmtop computer or directly onto your planner; or:
- Keep a small notebook and pen in your glove compartment expressly for recording mileage. It gives you all the mileage information in one place, and you needn't flip through other calendar notations in order to find the mileage information at tax time.

KEEP IT SIMPLE

1. Keep your car in good repair. There's nothing that will inconvenience you more than a breakdown on the way to or from a business meeting.

2. Invest in outfitting your car with useful office accessories. That way you can emerge from your car with papers collected in the correct file folders and everything as neatly organized as if you'd just stepped out of a real office.

3. If you're on the road a lot, membership in an automobile club is well worth the investment. Though a tow truck will come and get you if your car breaks down, have emergency supplies with you to tide you through until help arrives.

7

TECHNOLOGY THAT KEEPS YOU IN TOUCH

What's Ahead

91

Ten years ago the business traveler who was out of the office was often hard-pressed to keep up with everything that was going on. Pagers and faxes were the most commonly used forms of "instant" communication, and compared with the cell phones and e-mail options of today, there was actually nothing "instant" about them!

While many of the technological tools of today are still in their infancy in terms of development, we can see what is on the horizon, and what's coming, almost faster than we can write this, is the era of wireless communication. Today most of us still need to connect our computers in order to surf the 'Net; tomorrow (literally) we won't, and we'll all have Web access through our phones.

This chapter provides you with the information you need to be best equipped for doing business both today and in the future.

CELL PHONES AREN'T JUST FOR TALKING

Today's phones fall into three basic types: voice-only phones that manage to squeeze more bells and whistles into smaller and smaller packages; new voice-and-data phones with Internet microbrowsers; and "smart" phones that incorporate personal digital assistants (PDAs) along with microbrowsers.

Voice-Only Phones

If you temporarily opt for a voice-only phone, you'll find that they are now quite small (as light as 2.7 ounces), stylish, and come with lots of features including Caller ID, voice mail, and the ability to store frequently called phone numbers.

Voice-and-Data Phones with Internet Microbrowsers

Accessing the Internet via your phone will never be like sitting in front of a full-size computer where you can browse sites with amazing graphics and can truly search the entire Web. Early Web phones are bringing the Web to wireless users in the form of text-only information from an increasing number of Web sites that have opted to code their sites in a language suitable for the small screen. The types of Internet companies that are making themselves available for the tiny screens are those with time-critical data that you'd want to have available to you when you're on the phone. You'll be able to retrieve stock quotes, weather reports, make airline reservations, order dinner to pick up on the way home, and explore other similar content without connecting to a computer or modem.

Because it is laborious to use the number pad of a phone to communicate, some companies are offering a detachable keypad as an accessory. While this offers a solution to one problem, it creates another—it's one more thing to carry.

"Smart" Phones

These phones are part personal digital assistant (PDA) and part phone with microbrowser Internet access. An advantage to these devices is that they have the key capabilities of a PDA, which is more satisfactory than trying to send a message using the number pad of your telephone. They are designed for people who want portable management of information such as address books, calendars, and e-mail as well as corporate Intranet access and fax capability.

- At this point, to a greater or lesser degree, all digital cell phones are capable of sending and receiving text messages. This short messaging service (SMS) usually causes a phone to beep, and phones with miniature display screens will show the messages, each of which can be as long as 160 characters.

- Until wireless data receiving is the norm, it is still possible to retrieve your e-mail by phone. Many mobile phones can be connected to computers to allow data calls to the Internet. This function is also commonly used to send fax messages.

- You'll soon be able to "broadcast" a message to many co-workers about new information or the date and time of an upcoming meeting by making one call on your cell phone. (This may be one type of progress we'll regret when advertisers start broadcasting messages to us through our cell phones.)

- Remember that Web access isn't going to be free. If you opt for it, your phone company will bill it as an add-on service. Data calls are usually charged at a similar rate to voice calls, billed per minutes or per second. SMS is billed per message, and at this point each message would cost only a few cents.

While still in its infancy, use of a Web service by phone will be personalized with user-helpful information. You will be able to check on the weather, your e-mail, your stock portfolio, or the table availability at a nearby restaurant. For example, upon learning that a table is available, you'll be able to book it on your way down the street. It will mean convenient, there-when-you-need-it time savings for the business traveler.

PERSONAL DIGITAL ASSISTANTS AND LAPTOPS

Both of these items are becoming necessities for the business traveler.

Though some people still prefer a paper-based calendar system and separate address book, the convenience of the handheld lightweight computers is growing as they are becoming easier and easier to use. Now you can have one small unit that can hold your whole life, including everything from work-related lists to carpool phone numbers that you may still need even when you're away. Because they now interface with your office computer, you always have a backup of your calendar, your address book, and your "to do" list.

Laptop computers are to the business traveler what backpacks are to students. While you may not take it to every "class" you attend, they are an absolute necessity for getting your work done while you're on the road.

- Your laptop permits you to be efficient while away. When you can connect to the Internet, it permits you to do everything from checking on travel arrangements to staying on top of business deals with your office and being in touch with family. Though you may not always want to take it on overnight trips or when visiting offices where you'll have access to a computer, take it with you as often as possible to be able to best manage your time.

Though a laptop and a PDA serve very different purposes, the elements you consider when shopping for new ones are similar:

- Consider the resolution of the screen. Check to make certain the screen is visible to you in different circumstances.

- What is the battery life?

- What does the device weigh?

- PDA users may want one they can maneuver with one hand, and newer versions are offering software that fuses daily appointments with a "to do" list on one screen, a limitation of previous handheld computers.

- Laptop users should ask about wireless connectivity and memory. Also consider picking up a headset so that you can listen to audio Web sites or music on your laptop on planes.

WIRELESS OPTIONS

The world is going wireless. At this point, airports and hotels are putting in the infrastructure so that travelers can surf the Web without actually having to plug into anything. These systems operate in much the same way that a cordless phone works. Though you don't need to plug in, you do need to be within a certain range of the radio waves that are coming into the hotel or the airport "node" where a LAN (local area network) has been created.

Someone has to make money on this, and to gain access to this wireless connection, you need to purchase a networking card. Prices range from $100 to $200, and users pay a flat connection fee (at this time only $3.50) each time they log on.

Viruses can travel to your computer wirelessly just as easily as they can through the phone wires, so even though you may not feel "officially" connected, be sure not to open e-mail or attachments from those you don't know.

UNIFY YOUR MESSAGES

While the many options offered to business travelers as ways to keep in touch (fax, pager, several e-mail addresses, office phone, cell phone) are an improvement over the limited methods of the past, the very process of checking more than one e-mail address, several offices for messages, your cell phone messages, and looking for faxes is time-consuming. Consider how nice it would be to be able to make one call to check for all of your messages at the same time.

Now there are numerous "unified message services" that offer a variety of options for various monthly fees.

All services let users listen over the phone to their e-mail; the text is spoken by text-to-speech software, and the services will also play voice mail messages that have been forwarded. With most services, if a user wants to reply to an e-mail they dictate a response, and the service will send an e-mail reply that contains an audio file attachment with the dictated message.

Some services offer a find-me follow-me feature that bounces incoming calls from phone number to phone number to find you. However, you still have the opportunity to screen the call and decide whether or not you want to be "found."

Your fax machine can become obsolete with this service as those sending you a fax can send to a specific phone number, and you can have it read to you or access it from the Web site.

ALSO CONSIDER THESE TOOLS

When it comes to planning what else you need or want with you, you need to weigh the hassle of carrying extra business tools against the hassle of doing without them. There may be trips when your portable scanner works overtime as you gather information for a project, or there may be other trips when you would never unpack it. As you consider these items, select wisely:

- Consider a three-pound "pocket" cable-free printer; special attachments can turn it into a scanner.

- Just need a scanner? There is now one that is 1.5 by 11 inches. It interfaces with your notebook computer. It's great for travelers who need to scan documents and color photos in the field and store them in their notebook computers.

- Or what about a portable fax machine, scanner, and photocopier? This product folds to 1.25 by 12 inches and fits into a briefcase.

- Anyone who needs photos as part of their documentation for their work will find a digital camera to be helpful. Since you can download the pictures directly into your computer, it makes short work of integrating them into reports or presentations. Have along a spare memory card so that you needn't put everything on your laptop.

- If you do a lot of in-office presentations, you may want a portable PC projector for presentations. This device fits in a case no bigger than a briefcase, it is easy to set up, and because it offers a larger screen than your laptop, your clients will find your presentation easier to see and absorb.

- If you travel internationally a great deal, purchase a world phone that will let you stay in touch no matter where you are. Network coverage is better outside the U.S., so it is in addition to your regular cell phone, not instead of it.

- Buy or lease a two-way pager with coast-to-coast capability. These are soon going to be obsolete but right now they offer the advantage of a true keyboard and the ability to send and receive e-mail and text messages.

- A digital voice recorder with separate tracks (separate places to store messages) is the perfect penless notepad. Record quick notes to yourself while driving, or record driving directions to play back when you're en route.

- Drivers may be glad to have a global positioning satellite (GPS) receiver. You'll never get lost when driving again. The new voice-activated GPS receivers use satellite-navigation technology to create a door-to-door route map, estimate how long it should take to travel to your destination, and calculate mileage, which is great for an expense-report account. All are designed to sit on the dashboard, and some can be hot-linked to a handheld computer, which then displays route and location. (Technology is amazing, but keep those road maps in the car for the possibility of unexpected detours or of the car's computer going down.)

TECHNOLOGY COSTS

By this time, anyone who foots their own hotel telephone bill knows to reserve the hotel phone for incoming calls and use the lobby phone or your cell phone for outgoing calls. (The added charges for outgoing calls are costly.) More and more hotels are touting their new high-speed Internet access, but they're not advertising what they charge to use it. (According to the hotel industry, Internet usage should cost a bundle because it ties up a good number of phone lines for a prolonged period of time as businesspeople clear out their mailboxes and search the Web when they are restless.)

- Ask about:
  — Charges for local calls. These can range from free to $1.25 per minute.
  — Charges for credit card or 800-number calls; again, these can range from free to being billed like a local call. Some hotels don't charge for these calls until they go beyond a certain time limit.
  — Rates for Internet access. These vary greatly, from free access if the guest is using their own laptop to a per-minute

hook-up fee, to a flat $9.95 rate for 24-hour access to the high-speed line.

CRISIS AVOIDANCE

Computer and phone breakdowns are annoying at home, and even more so when on the road. Do what you can to minimize problems:

- Travel with a spare phone charger so you don't have to worry about remembering to pack it.

- If you travel beyond range of your Internet service provider, then be sure to use a service such as Yahoo or Excite that is accessible everywhere.

- Travel with a surge protector with extra outlets.

- Bring cables. You never know when you'll have to connect your laptop to a monitor or printer.

- Carry emergency disks with your startup program as well as your most used software.

- Make a backup copy of your presentation and/or the files you're working on so that you can reinstall them if necessary. Carry these separately.

- Back up your office computer before leaving for a trip.

- E-mail updated files to yourself so that you'll have a backup copy of the important information in your laptop.
- Make a separate note of tech support numbers to take with you. (Write this list in your notebook so that it's available to you even if your computer has crashed.)

KEEP IT SIMPLE

1. The organized business traveler will be one with top-flight technological equipment he or she knows how to use. You don't need all the gadgets and gizmos out there, but evaluate what you do need and then become proficient at using it.

2. Web-access telephones are going to become as common as sparrows in summertime. Stay up to date with what is available.

3. Back up whatever you can. If you can't back up your laptop on the road, e-mail important documents to yourself.

8

PACKING

WHAT'S AHEAD

Sensible Luggage
Equipment and Accessories
Trip Items that Belong in Your Briefcase or Handbag
Be Prepared
Protect Yourself
Creating a Good Packing List
Starter Packing Lists
Items You Might Not Have Thought Of
Packing
Garment Bag Packing
Additional Tips

Packing successfully for business can be achieved by following three simple principles:

1. Plan ahead for exactly what you will need.

2. Permanently pack items that always go with you.

3. Pare down. When it comes to travel, less is better than more. With the increase in 24-hour pharmacies and retail establishments that are open seven days a week, you will very likely be able to purchase anything you discover you need. (Travel to some foreign countries would be the exception to this.)

SENSIBLE LUGGAGE

The days of heavy hard-sided leather suitcases are gone. Whether you're traveling by plane, train, or car, your first priority should be to select luggage you can manage easily.

Currently a debate is raging over carry-on luggage. To stay within the size range, people have been overstuffing their cases, so they board the planes with heavy, hard-to-store bags that are snarling the system. It's slowing the boarding and exiting of passengers on all flights, and occasionally, people in aisle seats are getting hurt by falling bags as their owners try to put them into the overhead bin.

A reasonably packed carry-on offers the advantage of being able to disembark and go directly to your meeting, but if yours is going to be among the overstuffed, check it. Traveling with an unwieldy bag is stressful for anyone.

- Look for lightweight pieces that offer extra pockets for added flexibility.
- Most people own carry-on luggage of two types:
  - A small case on wheels with handles. These have been designed to be quite roomy, and the ample outside pockets expand your storage possibilities.
  - A garment bag. If you are traveling with clothing that you would prefer not to fold, then a sturdy garment bag may be your choice.

  A good luggage store will know the size limits of the various airlines, or visit the Web site of the carrier you fly most frequently to check for allowable dimensions.
- For a larger piece of luggage, shop for a sturdy, well-built suitcase that has wheels built into it. The soft-sided styles with zippered pockets on the exterior of the case provide lots of room for extra items.

EQUIPMENT AND ACCESSORIES

- Visit a good travel store to look for items that will make your travel life easier:

  _____ Collapsible skirt hanger.

  _____ Electric voltage adapters (if you travel internationally).

  _____ Hair dryer; ask if the hotel provides this.

  _____ Passport holder and/or money belt.

  _____ Sewing kit.

  _____ Small plastic bottles.

  _____ Travel alarm clock.

  _____ Travel iron; ask if the hotel provides an iron.

- Also look around to see what else has been invented. For example, a relatively new product that looks like a zippered pouch forces the air out of anything you're packing so that the items take up much less space than if simply folded. If you want to pack a coat or a pillow, you might look for one of these at your travel store. You may find other great products that fit your particular travel needs.

- Select a compact waterproof kit for toiletries that is large enough to hold what you need but small enough to be packed within your suitcase. One current model unfolds so that it can be hung from a towel bar in your hotel room, permitting you easy access to everything from aftershave and moisturizer to makeup and shampoo without fully unpacking. If you're checking your luggage, see if you can fit this into your carry-on, or wrap it in a large plastic bag so that all the tossing and bouncing your suitcase receives won't result in leaks that go through to your clothing.

- Purchase luggage tags if you don't already own them. Some are designed so that you have to take the tag apart in order to find the name and address. This is for security reasons—you don't want a bag with your name and address advertising the fact that you are away from home. If you work somewhere outside the home, another way to safeguard your security while still labeling your bag is to put your work address on the tag. That way the bag is labeled, but the security of your home isn't at risk.

TRIP ITEMS THAT BELONG IN YOUR BRIEFCASE OR HANDBAG

If you're traveling by plane, there will be certain items that you will want to have accessible, either in your briefcase or handbag. (Also review Chapter 5, The Ever-Ready Briefcase.)

_____ Your itinerary (also pack a copy and leave copies with someone at home and at the office).

_____ Tickets.

_____ Passport (for foreign travel).

_____ Identification (domestic travel).

_____ Extra cash, including dollar bills for tipping.

_____ Credit cards and checkbook or travelers' checks.

_____ Valuables or jewelry (keep to a minimum).

_____ Flight guide, in case of rescheduling.

_____ Calendar/address book or personal digital assistant.

_____ Nasal spray (for those who have ear pressure problems on airplanes).

_____ Ear plugs; these can be helpful in blocking out plane sounds, but you may also find them handy if you're in a hotel room where you hear everything happening in the hallway.

- If you're checking your luggage, then pack an extra set of underwear and a fresh shirt or blouse in your carry-on bag. While the odds are in your favor that you and your suitcase will arrive together, this safety precaution will let you get by for a day if your bag is delayed.

- The new fashionability of shawls that are warm and lightweight has increased the comfort of female travelers. If you haven't thought of it before, travel with a shawl so that you can cover up easily when the plane is cool.

- Dry air on a plane can be countered with moisturizer and/or hand lotion. Keep travel-size containers of these in your handbag or briefcase.

- If you have a long flight or will be running right to a meeting, consider carrying toothbrush and paste as well as towelettes for cleaning up a bit. Men might carry a disposable razor for a quick shave.

- If you plan to work on the flight, you will want your laptop and any relevant files.

- Flight time also offers free time. Most people like to take along a novel, some magazines, or your "on the go" reading file for spending some pleasurable time while traveling.

- Good ideas often come when you have downtime. To keep track of your thoughts, be sure you have a pocket notebook, a digital recorder, or your personal digital assistant.

BE PREPARED

Some business trips come up at a moment's notice. The organized business traveler will be able to depart at a moment's notice by doing the following:

- Keep your toiletries kit permanently packed:
  - Invest in an extra toothbrush, shaver, comb and brush, and travel-size toothpaste, shampoo, lotion, and aspirin that can be left in the kit at all times.

— Transfer special items like your facial cleanser or moisturizer into small plastic bottles (available at travel and drugstores). Fill only three-quarters of the way full to allow for changes in air pressure. At the end of each trip, refill any that are getting low.

— Try to travel with as few spillables as possible. Those liquids that you do take with you should be placed in a plastic bag. If a bottle should leak or spill, the liquid will spread no farther than the plastic bag.

— Use a transparent bag for your cosmetics to make it easier to put your hands on the product you need.

— Within the toiletries bag, keep related items together. Retrieval is easier when toothbrush, toothpaste and floss, facial cleanser and moisturizer, and shampoo and conditioner are all compartmentalized.

• When you run out of anything that you intend to keep permanently packed, write a big note to yourself and get it on your "to do" list as soon as possible. You may even have time to pick up items while traveling.

• If you travel frequently and exercise regularly while away, purchase shoes that you can keep permanently packed. Dedicate a set of exercise clothing to travel as well. After laundering, the exercise clothing can be immediately repacked.

- Make a habit of keeping your clothing in good order. Buttons should be replaced, hems should be resewn, scuffed shoes should be polished before putting them back into the closet. If a business trip is scheduled at the last minute, all of your clothing is ready to go.

- Buy a folding coatrack. Whether you have three days or thirty minutes notice that you have to leave on a trip, you can display the clothing you may want to take with you. This system makes it easy to coordinate jackets, pants or skirts, and shirts or tops.

PROTECT YOURSELF

- Keep permanently packed a spare pair of prescription eyewear or a copy of your current prescription. If your glasses get lost or broken, you have another pair with you or you can get one made quickly.

- Also take along a photocopy of any prescription medicines that you may need.

CREATING A GOOD PACKING LIST

Like a good grocery list, a packing list guarantees that you will remember to take everything you intended to. Photocopy the basic packing lists that are provided, and use them as "starter" lists each time you leave on a trip. In addition, here are ways to tailor the list so that you are prepared for each trip you take:

- Before each trip, check the Internet for the weather in the place you're visiting. Once you have temperature and climate conditions, adapt the list to accommodate the weather that is anticipated for the area. You still need to think "layers." Whether it's a sweater in case beastly hot weather turns cool, or a coat despite not-as-cold-as-expected winter temperatures, you will pack so that you can dress according to the weather.

- Invest in a nylon rain jacket that can be folded and carried in your briefcase or a tote.

- Permanently pack gloves and a lightweight winter scarf and hat. If a September night takes on a chill, you don't need to suffer.

- Travel is no time to test out new outfits. If you're uncomfortable, you have no options. And if a winter trip to a warm climate necessitates taking summer clothing, be certain to try on everything in advance.

- Women should pack interchangeable basics in sophisticated neutrals such as taupe, white, gray, or black; brightly colored tops and accessories brighten your overall look.

- In many circumstances, sweater sets serve the same function as jackets, and they are easier to pack.

- Because shoes are heavy and bulky, plan to take as few pairs as possible. Those you do take should be comfortable ones!

- The more scheduled stops you have, the fewer clothes you'll need. By rinsing out washables at night, and sending jackets, slacks, or a skirt to the hotel cleaners, you can rotate two or three outfits and still look professional, pressed, and pulled together.

- If business takes you to a foreign country, ask in advance about local custom. Some countries frown upon sleeveless dresses, shorts, or very short skirts.

- In warm climates, natural fibers are best; synthetic clothing doesn't breathe as well.

- Clothing treated with UV protection is now available for those who are concerned about sunburns; if that doesn't interest you, at least shop for opaque clothing that will offer some protection.

- Consider anything special you may need for this particular trip: Are you on any special medications? Is it your great aunt's birthday, and you'll want to have her phone number so you can call from the road? Are you attending a black-tie event and need to pack all the associated items as well as a tux or a gown?

STARTER PACKING LISTS

Use the following list to get started:

_____ belts	_____ hats	_____ sleepwear
_____ blouses	_____ jackets	_____ slippers
_____ boots	_____ jeans	_____ slips
_____ bras	_____ raincoat	_____ socks
_____ coat	_____ robe	_____ stockings
_____ dresses	_____ scarves	_____ suits
_____ exercise gear	_____ shirts	_____ sweaters
_____ gloves	_____ shoes	_____ swimsuit
_____ gowns	_____ skirts	_____ ties
	_____ slacks	_____ underwear

The items on this list should be permanently packed in your toiletries kit. Replenish after every trip:

_____ aftershave	_____ deodorant
_____ brush and comb	_____ feminine needs
_____ collar stays	_____ hair accessories
_____ cottonballs	_____ hair dryer
_____ cotton swabs	_____ hair gel or spray
_____ creams, lotions	_____ makeup
_____ dental floss	_____ manicure items

_____ mouthwash	_____ shower cap
_____ perfume (or scented lotion)	_____ sunblock
	_____ talc
_____ shampoo, conditioner	_____ toothbrush and paste
_____ shaving kit and razor	_____ tweezers

The following items should also be permanently packed:

_____ Bandage strips (assorted).

_____ Basic medicines (painkiller/fever reducer, antacid tablets, cold remedies, cough drops, etc.).

_____ First-aid ointment.

_____ Insect repellent.

_____ Thermometer.

And don't forget:

_____ Alarm clock.

_____ Flashlight.

_____ Hat—whether it's a baseball cap or a packable sunhat, many health-conscious people today don't like being caught without something to protect their head from the sun.

_____ Overnight mail forms/envelopes.

_____ Safety pins.

_____ Sewing kit and scissors.

_____ Shoehorn.

_____ Stain stick.

_____ Stamps.

_____ Sunglasses.

_____ Umbrella.

Each trip you will need to pack:

_____ Vitamins.

_____ Prescription medicines.

Working from the above items, create your own packing list of the items appropriate to you. Make photocopies or work from your computer, and use the list as a check-off system for each time you pack.

ITEMS YOU MIGHT NOT HAVE THOUGHT OF

We're becoming so dependent on technology that it seems the world is ending if we can't use our phone or our laptop. To keep your life running electronically, purchase and permanently pack:

- An extra phone charger.
- An extra battery pack for your PC.
- While most hotel rooms are now equipped to make Internet access easy, it doesn't hurt to have along one of the travel kits that will provide the wires and connections that will aid in your logging on from your hotel room.

PACKING

- Don't overpack. Unless you're going to a remote area where it will be difficult to restock, pack what you think you'll need, but limit the "just in case" items.

- In addition to the clothing hanging on your "packing" coatrack, lay out clothing that is folded, not hung (sweaters, tops, underwear, accessories).

- Pack a softsided suitcase on a hard surface, so that you can fill the bag evenly and completely.

- Fold clothing as few times as possible. Folding clothing that is still packaged in the plastic from the dry cleaner works well, too.

- Pack with tissue paper to minimize wrinkling. Save tissue paper that comes in gift packages and from the dry cleaner.

- Women may want to spray the tissue paper with a fragrance. When the clothing is unpacked, it has a pleasant smell to it.

- Place a dryer sheet in one of the pockets of your suitcase. Your clothing will smell good, and if any of your clothing suffers from static cling, the dryer sheet can be used to cure it.

- Heavier, more wrinkle-resistant items (sweaters, robe, jeans) belong on the bottom of the suitcase.

- Rolling clothing is an effective way to reduce wrinkling and save space. However, an equally effective way to manage the space in the suitcase is a "layering" method I use: alternate layers of clothing as you pack. First pack a layer from left to right so that the top of the coat or jeans stretches out of the suitcase to the left. Next, stretch a layer out to the right. Fold the layer on the left back over the layer that is stretched out to the right, and repeat on the other side. This method provides a fatter fold and, therefore, a less-defined crease in the clothing.

- Store underwear and hosiery in separate transparent plastic bags, and tuck them into the corner of your suitcase.

- Pack items inside one another: socks and shoehorn can go inside shoes, for example.

- With the exception of light, thin sandals or beach shoes, each shoe should be packed in a separate plastic bag and placed along the hinge of the suitcase so that when the bag is standing upright the shoes are on the bottom. By packing them individually, the bulky items within your suitcase can be better distributed.

- Fill the corners of the bag with rolled-up belts, tights, and scarves. By artfully filling the space, everything you've packed is protected from shifting and sliding within the case.

- If you know what you are doing upon arrival, put the items you'll need first on the top of the case.

- Take an extra oversize plastic bag or two for laundry or damp gym clothes.

- If you're taking a good number of skirts, consider bringing along a collapsible skirt hanger.

- Pack a lightweight tote as a handy carry-all for day excursions or for carrying home additional work or purchases.

GARMENT BAG PACKING

If you need to arrive with a wrinkle-free suit for a major business presentation, a garment bag is your best choice.

- If the suit is just back from the dry cleaner, then in all likelihood, it is carefully packed and ready to go. If not, ask your dry cleaner to provide you with tissue and the type of hanger that has cardboard on the cross piece:

— Fold tissue over the bar, and then hang your pants over it.

— Now drape tissue over the hanger's shoulders. Hang your shirt or blouse and stuff the sleeves with tissue.

— Next hang your jacket over that, pulling the shirt or blouse sleeves through the jacket sleeves.

— Check the overall look and be certain the jacket isn't crushing the shirt collar.

— Finally slip a plastic dry-cleaning bag over the whole suit and slip it carefully into the garment bag. The clothing will hold its shape because of the tissue, and the plastic will let the clothing hang free without friction. You should arrive and have a suit that looks fresh from the cleaners.

• Shoes, toiletries, and accessories should be placed in any outside pockets, or pack them at the bottom of your tote bag.

• Don't overstuff a garment bag. Hanging items will arrive mussed and wrinkled.

ADDITIONAL TIPS

• Save your receipts for any clothing you primarily use for travel. Claim limits are now up to $2,500 per bag, and some airlines require receipts to get full value.

- If you must check your luggage, tie a brightly colored piece of cloth or a ribbon on your suitcase handle. That way you'll know exactly which bag is yours as the luggage arrives on the baggage carrousel.

- Write your name, address, and telephone number on an index card and pack it. For each trip, also add a copy of your latest itinerary with dates and telephone numbers. If your bag is lost or stolen and the luggage tags are removed, you've provided a way for someone to locate you.

- Carry a photograph of your luggage in your briefcase. If your bag is lost or stolen, you have the perfect ID, and it will save you time when you have to fill out forms.

- Take along a few extra plastic bags and a roll of cellophane tape. The bags will come in handy when packing up laundry, spillables, and shoes. The tape may save the day by holding up a drooping hem or removing lint from your suit.

- The simplest way to repack while away is to refold each item and place it into the suitcase as you finish with it.

KEEP IT SIMPLE

1. Keep a permanently packed toiletries kit so that you don't even have to think "pack comb" before you leave.

2. Create a packing list and work from it to be sure you have what you need. Pack what you need but don't overpack.

3. Work from one color family so that you can minimize the additional clothing and accessories that you take with you.

PART THREE

ON THE

ROAD

9
AIR TRAVEL

WHAT'S AHEAD

Planning Ahead
Booking Your Flight
Plane Necessities
The Safe Skies
Preflight Prep
Airport Parking
Backup Plans
If You Are Bumped
In Flight
On Arrival

On my way home from a business conference, I got involved in an interesting conversation with the gate agents while I was waiting to board the plane, and when it was time to board, I had neglected to pick up my carry-on bag. Once onboard, I realized I'd left my luggage. I started working my way back through the passengers boarding the flight only to be met in the jetway by one of the agents with whom I'd been speaking. Once she realized what had happened, she was kind enough to carry it down to meet me.

This experience reminded me that kindness is almost always repaid, and at no time is this more important than when traveling. Though flights may be delayed or the planes may be overly crowded, try to relax and be as good-natured as you can about the whole process. The one who will primarily benefit from this attitude is you.

PLANNING AHEAD

- Try to fly regularly on one airline. You'll be able to benefit from building up miles and can either use them for bringing family members along or upgrading to business or first class. Many business travelers enjoy using them for the upgrade. Not only is it a more comfortable way to travel, but they find that they are more likely to meet potential clients in business or first class, making it an excellent networking opportunity.

- Maximize your bonus miles by finding out how else you can accrue mileage. Some credit cards, rental car companies, supermarkets, and hotels award mileage, and by patronizing them, your miles will add up even faster.

- Join the club of the airline you fly most frequently. Membership status offers upgrade benefits, a nice lounge where you can wait between flights, and help if flights are cancelled. Some clubs have conference rooms and office facilities for business travelers; a few have showers so that you can freshen up after a long or an overnight flight.

- Write down all frequent flyer numbers on a small card to keep in your wallet and note them in your handheld computer or organizer as well. That way you don't have to travel with a card for each airline.

- If you're meeting colleagues at the airport, go online for a printout of the airport layout. Then you can agree on an exact meeting place within what are usually very expansive buildings.

BOOKING YOUR FLIGHT

- Some people travel at night to keep days free for meetings; other people find it more effective to book an early morning flight, the time of day when fewer flights are more likely to be delayed. The early morning hour also means you'll have more flight options if your plane is cancelled and you need to rebook.

- Ask about on-time arrival. Every flight is assigned an on-time performance rating of from 1 (on schedule only 10 percent of the time) to 10 (on schedule 100 percent of the time). If you find a particular flight is chronically late, look for an alternative.

- If you have long legs, check out the configuration of different planes and ask for seats with the most leg room. In coach these are generally the bulkhead seats and the emergency exit rows. (Families generally request bulkhead seats, so you may prefer the emergency exit rows.)

- Ask for a seat toward the front. It will speed your departure from the plane, particularly helpful if you have a connecting flight.

- Most business travelers prefer the aisle seats because sitting on the aisle also makes it easy to get out quickly. However, if you expect to sleep during most of a late-night flight, try to book a window seat.

- Choose your aisle seat based on handedness. Lefties are best seated on the right side of the plane; right-handers are better off on the left side. This puts your active arm in the aisle where you need to be alert to bumps from the cart, but at least you're not constantly jostled by your neighbor.

- Request a special meal at the time you book your flight. Special meals tend to be fresher and healthier.

- If you use a travel agent, let him or her know your seat and meal preference.

PLANE NECESSITIES

- Have with you:
  - OAG flight guide.
  - Telephone number of your after-hours travel agent.
  - Cell phone.
  - Bottle of water.
  - Lip balm.
  - Snack food (fruit, carrot sticks, crackers, pretzels).
  - Motion sickness tablet (just in case).
  - For longer flights, an inflatable cervical pillow or a hand towel to roll and put behind your neck to decrease aches from sleeping.
  - Premoistened towelette to freshen up at the end of the flight.
  - Reading material, either business magazines or a great novel.

- Women also like to have:
  - Shawl or sweater and warm socks, in case it's cold on the plane.
  - Moisturizer and hand lotion.

THE SAFE SKIES

Airline travel is an exceedingly safe form of travel, but sometimes when you are flying for business, you need to take an airline on which you haven't flown.

- To check the safety records of any airline, check this Federal Aviation Administration website: *www.faa.gov/agc/enforcement/index.htm*. A history of repeated fines would suggest chronic problems with a particular airline. See if there isn't another carrier that flies into the area you're visiting.

- Foreign airlines that fly into the U.S. must comply with all U.S. safety guidelines, but if you are flying internationally on planes that don't land in the United States, log on to the International Aviation Safety Assessment Web page, *www.faa.gov/avr/iasa/index.htm*, to check the safety record of foreign airlines.

- In general, the riskiest part of the flight is the ascent and descent, so if you have a choice, book one long flight rather than several shorter ones. It also saves time.

- Take the airlines' messages about seat belts seriously and wear your seat belt when you aren't moving about the cabin. Statistically, you are far more likely to be hurt because of falling during turbulence than you are from being in a plane crash.

PREFLIGHT PREP

- Travel in business attire. Looking professional will make a difference in how you are treated while traveling, and you're prepared if your plane is delayed and you have to run directly to a client meeting. If you opt not to travel in business clothes, have something businesslike in your carry-on in case you need it.
- If you have carry-on luggage, be sure it meets the size qualifications for the airline you're flying. Check the airline Web site for specifications.
- Always call to verify your flight and departure gate before leaving for the airport.
- Never leave for the airport without some cash. If the ATMs at the airport aren't in service or you don't have time to find one, you'll be happy to have enough cash on you to cover at least 24 hours.
- Allow plenty of time to get to the airport. Traffic tie-ups are common in major metropolitan areas, and you are better off being there too early than too late.

- If you're carrying videocassettes for a presentation, don't let them go through the airport metal detector.

- If you are a club member of the airline you're flying, check in at the club. The staff will be helpful in working out any problems, and you can wait in comfort until it's time to report to the gate.

- When you check in, verify that the agent has your frequent flyer number in the computer.

- When returning to the airport in a rented car, drop your luggage off and check it curbside. Then return the car. That way you're not lugging heavy baggage on the shuttle coming back to the airport.

AIRPORT PARKING

Whether or not to drive to the airport depends on the time of year, convenience of parking, and the prices charged. Arriving at your home airport and bypassing cab lines and shuttle buses to go directly to your car is a wonderful feeling, but not if your car is buried under four feet of snow or the price charged is exorbitant. At your airport, find out the following:

- Is there covered parking reasonably close to the terminal, and how much will it cost per day to leave it there? Fees range from $7 for outlying lots in less-traveled airports to $21 per day around major metropolitan centers. If you're gone for more than a day or two, it may be difficult to justify the cost. An increasing number of airports are working to complete rail systems to the airports to increase convenience in getting to the terminals. Bay Area Rapid Transit (BART) already connects San Francisco to its airport, and JFK and Newark will soon have systems in place, too.

- Is there a number to call for information about which lots are full and which still have spaces available?

- Does your airport offer valet parking? Some airports now have someone who will take your car and bring it back to you, all for a cost, of course.

- Does your company pay for corporate spaces? Some airports lease reserved, nearby spaces for corporate clients. You may be eligible for one of these preferred parking spaces.

- How quickly can you arrive at the airport and locate a parking place? Technology is making the "where to park" and "how to pay" issues easier. Some airports are installing electronic signage that tells drivers the whereabouts of available parking; others are establishing systems where drivers can swipe their credit cards to pay to minimize exit hassles.

- Does your airport have any off-site parking that offers a decent alternative? Entrepreneurs saw a need for competition to ease airports' problems with overcrowding. Call and ask for brochures. Shuttle buses will get you to the airport, though some offer valet parking and will bring your car to you at the airport. Others offer free car washes and detailing while you're gone. Their lounges may feature airline info update screens, fax and copy machines. Discounts are frequently available to repeat patrons.

- If you drive:

    — At the airport try to consistently park your car in one area of the parking lot. This will make it easier to find it on your return.

    — Park in well-lit, well-trafficked areas.

    — Don't leave valuables in the car.

    — Use a Club or similar type of security device.

    — Avoid parking in uncovered lots during the winter. A snow-storm could completely bury your car and make your coming home less than welcome.

    — Avoid bringing your car during holiday periods when parking can be hard to find.

BACKUP PLANS

- If your flight is delayed or cancelled, go to the phones or use your cell phone. The counter agents will be overwhelmed by upset travelers; the phone agents will be able to focus on exactly what you need in order to change travel plans.

- Have your flight guide with you and know what secondary airports are nearby. That way if you need to rebook, you can point the person helping you toward a workable solution rather than having to let them think of alternatives.

- If you're going to miss a meeting because of a delay, report to your airline club and ask about teleconferencing facilities. They may be able to provide you and any co-workers with a conference room so that you can attend the meeting by phone if not in person.

- As a passenger, know your rights if your plane is unduly delayed: Your airline is obligated to pick up the tab for any additional expense in getting you to your intended destination via another carrier. This rule applies to other nonstop flights to your final destination as well as connecting flights.

- Stranded at the airport? That can be upsetting, but before becoming enraged, consider your options. Is there any creative way to leave (fly to a different airport and then try to get home? Use a car service to get you to another airport or to get you home after flying to another airport? Switch to another mode of transportation such as a train? etc.). If not, think how to make the best of being stranded in an airport:

  — Call an old friend.

  — Visit an airport bookshop and buy a new book you've been dying to read to make the best of your waiting time.

— Investigate where you might be able to check your carry-on luggage, and then you can take an energizing walk through the airport unencumbered.

— Some airports offer diversions. If you don't know of any, check with airport personnel, other passengers, or a clerk at one of the shops. Las Vegas has more than 1,200 slot machines; Denver International Airport has an onsite chiropractor; some airports have first-class restaurants or ones in connecting hotels; in Chicago it isn't too difficult to get to the O'Hare Hilton to pay a per-visit fee to use their health club; and Miami International Hotel has a rooftop area with a wonderful view as well as a sauna, gym, pool, and a rooftop running track.

— Book an even later flight and go out to explore the city.

When this happened to me, I *wished* I had been on a business trip! Instead, we were on a family trip to Canada with my three children, including seven-year-old twins, and instead of reaching our destination in a few hours, a series of delays caused by poor weather conditions, mechanical problems, and rerouting the trip took 24 hours! Two things saved the day: I stayed calm when few other passengers were because I knew that would help my family stay calm, too, and I encouraged the kids to turn the experience into an "adventure." It worked!

IF YOU ARE BUMPED

Your work schedule and your company's policy on what happens to travel vouchers (offered as compensation by the airlines) if you get bumped from a flight will influence how you feel about being bumped. Though many companies let employees use the travel vouchers themselves, business travelers often can't afford to miss the flight.

If, however, you're on the way home from a business trip (or know there's another flight within the hour) and wouldn't mind a free plane ticket, ask to be put on the voluntary "bump" list. You may get a free trip out of it.

IN FLIGHT

- On departure from home, carry a large preaddressed "overnight" envelope with you to mail any work completed on the flight back to your office. Coming home, collect all work in a file folder for that purpose.

- Try not to check presentation materials. If you have a large portfolio presentation case, try to arrive at the gate promptly and ask gate personnel if you can put the case in the first-class coat closet before everyone else boards.

- If sitting in an aisle seat, pay attention to what goes in the overhead bin above you. Aisle seat passengers have been injured when overhead items have come down on them.

- When the plane takes off, change your watch to the time of your destination.

- To fight dehydration, drink a glass of water for every hour on the plane, and avoid alcohol and caffeine.

- On long flights get up each hour and walk around. It is reenergizing and will help fight fatigue.

- Open food packets (salad dressing, half-and-half, etc.) toward the seat in front of you. If there is a spray, it goes on the seat in front of you, not your business suit.

- Relieve cabin pressure earaches by taking a decongestant prior to the flight, and using a nasal spray in each nostril before descent. Swallowing regularly and chewing gum can also help. Some people find relief by holding paper cups over their ears during descent.

ON ARRIVAL

- Instead of waiting for your luggage first, go directly to the car rental counter. In some airports, your luggage will be arriving on the baggage claim conveyor belt just about the time you get there. You've minimized waiting time, and you haven't had to drag your bags with you.

- While the majority of bags make it safely to their destination, now and then they do get lost. Here's what to do:

  — Proceed immediately to the airline claim office and fill out a lost bags report.

  — Get vouchers or commitments for immediate necessities: shaving items, toothbrush and paste, deodorant, etc.

  — Make sure the airline has an easy way to contact you once the bag is found. This is easier if you're returning home; if you're in a new town, then your cell phone number, a beeper, or the hotel number should all be left so that they can definitely locate you as quickly as possible so delivery can be arranged.

KEEP IT SIMPLE

1. To get the best treatment while traveling, travel in business attire, and be courteous to all around you.

2. Always travel with the OAG flight guide and emergency numbers. As all business travelers know, rebooking flights is very common.

3. Relax and take what happens in stride. You have very little control over when and whether your flight takes off, so your primary goals while traveling by air should be focused on how to amuse yourself while waiting and while flying.

10

MANAGING JET LAG

WHAT'S AHEAD

The Impossible Dream?
Straddling the Time Zones
Flying Right
Making the Adjustment
Other Remedies

Most people who travel through several time zones suffer some form of jet lag. Unfortunately, business travelers can rarely afford to dedicate a couple of days just to adjust to the time. Nor can they afford to suffer the symptoms associated with jet lag, which can include fatigue, insomnia, lack of alertness, irritability, disorientation, headaches, digestive unrest, and lightheadedness. Most symptoms aren't severe, but they can certainly be unsettling as you leave your hotel to start a round of business meetings.

Jet lag is a disruption of our human circadian rhythm or the body's sleep/wake cycle. Receptors in the brain regulate the body clock that controls when to wake up and when to fall asleep. When those receptors become out of phase with daylight hours, there is a delay while the brain tries to readjust.

If you're a Californian who has flown to New York, your body knows very well that 7 A.M. Eastern Time is actually 4 A.M. in Los Angeles. Imagine how your poor body feels when you drag it from Los Angeles to London where it's eight hours earlier! Utterly confused. For someone's body to make a full and normal adjustment, it takes approximately a day per time zone; after three days, a New Yorker can have his body clock reset to California time, for example.

Travelers will testify that it is harder to travel west to east, as this crunches the day. It is more difficult to fall asleep at an earlier bedtime and then get up earlier as well. Those traveling east to west find it is easier because it lengthens the day and the body adjusts more easily.

Theories about how to cure jet lag are numerous. They range from "light" cures to various herbal remedies. Because nothing has yet been proven to be 100 percent effective for everyone, this chapter provides information on some of the remedies found to be effective for some people as well as general advice on managing your physical condition despite jumping from time zone to time zone.

THE IMPOSSIBLE DREAM?

Starting your trip well-rested may seem an impossible goal for most business travelers, but studies show that those who aren't tired when the trip begins do better than those who start out with a sleep deficit.

STRADDLING THE TIME ZONES

Easterners who travel west often keep East Coast hours even when working on the West Coast. "My office opens at nine a.m., so at six a.m. (Pacific Time) I need to be on the phone with them." This is all well and good, but if you choose this schedule for your business trips, you need to try to sleep (and to some extent, eat) according to your home time zone hours as well.

- Rather than staying at a restaurant with a group until 11 P.M., excuse yourself when you can and go back to your hotel room.
- Try to avoid late-night meetings if you are an easterner flying west.
- Try to avoid breakfast meetings if you are a westerner flying east.
- If you're traveling through three time zones or more, then the above advice must change. The greater the time change, the more important it is to adapt to the new time as soon as possible.

FLYING RIGHT

- If you can, start shifting your body clock prior to the trip. If you're flying west to east, try going to bed earlier and waking up earlier for several days in advance of the trip. (In addition to helping you adjust to the new time, your earlier wake-up gives you a jump-start on the day.) Flying east to west makes it more difficult to shift in advance as most people can't afford to sleep later on a workday. However, if you have the luxury of a weekend before your trip, then use your east-west flight as an excuse to stay in bed a little longer.

- When traveling internationally and flying east (to Europe or beyond from the U.S.), book a night flight and then try to sleep as much as you can during the flight. Once you arrive during the day, spend time outside during the daylight hours. Natural light cues your body to the new environment and helps reset your body clock.

- Flying west (Japan, China), American travelers will do best taking a flight that arrives at night so that they can go to sleep when they get there. To begin to adjust to the new time, sleep at the beginning of the flight and stay awake later on so that you'll be tired by the time you arrive.

- When you board the plane, reset your watch for the time of the city you're visiting. Then do the best you can to let this new time dictate your activities. If it's daytime there, try to stay up (napping briefly if necessary); if it is night, sleep as much as you can, rousing yourself when it would be morning there. (An eye mask will make it easier to sleep on the plane.)

- Exercise, both in the air (isometrics as well as an occasional stroll down the aisle) and upon arrival, will stimulate your system and help you make the time adjustment.

- Dehydration contributes to jet lag, and experts recommend that you drink eight ounces of water for each hour you're in the plane. Carrying your own water bottle and requesting an aisle seat will make this easier.

- Splash water on your face occasionally. Planes are very dehydrating, which affects how you feel physically and a dry throat and nose lead to an increased likelihood of infection since dry membranes are more susceptible.

- Avoid caffeine and alcohol. Both increase dehydration, which throws your body even more out of whack.

- If you're arriving at your destination in the evening, don't sleep on the plane.

- If you can afford the time, fly in a day or so early to see some sights and adjust to the new time zone. This is particularly helpful on a foreign visit where you're going through several time zone changes.

MAKING THE ADJUSTMENT

- If you arrive at your destination early in the day, try to stay up until 8 P.M. or so local time. If you arrive late in the day, go to sleep by midnight locally. By adapting to the time change as quickly as possible, you'll find that you will sleep better.

- Maintain your home routine regarding exercising and eating habits. Your body is already under stress trying to adapt to the new time, so try to eat moderately and maintain an exercise regimen so that your body is being treated somewhat normally.

- While most businesspeople need to keep a mental clock on what is happening in the home office, this makes adjustment to the new time more difficult. Some businesspeople use watches that note two time zones so that they have a quick way to check on what time it is at home without having to keep track of it mentally.

OTHER REMEDIES

There are a lot of theories about what cures jet lag. Some of those that are touted but not fully proven include the following:

- Melatonin is perhaps the best known of the recent cures. Melatonin is a substance that is produced by the human body at night, and it tricks the body into resetting the natural sleep/awake cycle. While some swear by melatonin, it is banned in Britain and not regulated by the FDA because it is classified as a nutritional supplement and has not proven to be effective for all who try it. If you are interested in trying it, check with your doctor first. Also, get recommendations on a reputable supplement manufacturer to insure quality. Because melatonin has to do with resetting the body clock, it is not like popping a sleeping pill; you need specific advice regarding both quantity and timing for it to possibly be effective. These are good questions to pose to your doctor.

- Vitamin supplements are put forth as a remedy by some researchers who believe that the abuse to your body begins with the prolonged period on a plane and that the body's nutritional needs are drained during flight. B12 and vitamin C are two vitamins that some find helpful. Inactivity also leads to a depletion of potassium, but a banana or a glass of orange juice can remedy this. Again, check with your doctor to learn more.

- In years past, alternating feasting and fasting was thought to help relieve jet lag. Today the best thing to keep in mind is that high protein meals are more difficult to digest and stimulate wakefulness; carbohydrates promote sleep.

- Aromatherapy and massage are two treatments about which it would be difficult to complain! This is being offered at spas and hotels to help with jet lag, and indeed, if you take time to pamper yourself, you'll likely feel better, which in turn will help you adjust to the new time.

- The "light cure" is a new theory being put forward by some. Hotels are beginning to install light boxes to be used to help get over jet lag. Two Harvard scientists believe that only outdoor light helps, and they recommend exposure to five hours of sunlight per day.

- For some people, a prescription remedy may be the preferred choice. Ask your doctor about using one of the newly developed sleeping pills that have just come on the market. Because they are effective and don't cause grogginess, they are being used for jet lag by travelers who want to sleep while on the flight but need to awaken ready for business.

- If you read about a cure and it costs you nothing (going out in the light) or involves money you're willing to spend (for a massage?), then give it a try. But watch out for bogus claims and be careful about herbs and medicines for jet lag. One can be hard on your wallet, the second can be hard on your body.

The true solution to jet lag may lie in making the mental leap to adjusting to the new time. Seasoned travelers say that willing yourself into life in the new time zone is absolutely critical to success. While there may be times when you're very sleepy during the day or wakeful at night, a moderate diet, exercise, and not taking lengthy naps will help you "sleep when the natives sleep." And if you do find yourself up in the middle of the night, take out a book or magazine (don't try to work, because it's stimulating) and read and relax for a little while before trying to go back to sleep.

KEEP IT SIMPLE

1. For short trips back and forth across the U.S., most business travelers find it easier to remain on their own time, making adjustments as needed for mealtime meetings when you have to accommodate the time zone schedule of the people you're visiting.

2. For trips across several time zones or for trips of longer duration, adjust your watch and start living on the schedule of the place you're visiting as soon as you board the plane. If it's night there, go to sleep. If it's daytime, try to stay awake as much as possible. Eat lightly so that your body has one less thing to "worry" about.

3. Drink lots of water and do isometrics in your plane seat. Avoiding dehydration and keeping your blood flowing are two components to successful adjustment to a new time zone.

11

THE HOTEL:

YOUR SEARCH FOR
OVERNIGHT COMFORT

WHAT'S AHEAD

Business travel can be interesting, but moving from place to place to accomplish your work is very tiring. One of the few things you can do to take good care of yourself is to find ways to have a peaceful evening and a good night's sleep. The key to this, of course, is pleasant lodging. Whether you're driving from town to town and staying in motels along the way or flying in and out of major cities where a midtown hotel is most appropriate for your needs, here's some advice on finding the best place to stay and making it your home away from home.

THE RIGHT HOTEL

If you are traveling to major cities, try to stay at a full-service hotel with bellmen, gym or a pool, 24-hour room service, and business floors that offer special amenities ranging from office centers with copiers and fax facilities to free continental breakfasts. Being located in a hotel that makes your travel life easy pays off in providing you with more time to work while you're there and less stress because trip-related tasks are getting done.

Atmospheric hotels are terrific for weekend getaways, but unless you select a hotel that has been recently updated, you may find that "atmosphere" isn't much fun when you need to send a fax or would appreciate hotel voice mail service. In addition, follow these suggestions:

- Consider location. If you're arriving by car, easy access to the highway is important; if you're arriving by air, then select a hotel or motel that is conveniently located near your client's office or your meeting site.

- Visit the Web. Hotel sites as well as sites such as *Travelweb.com* provide pictures of rooms at major hotels. Web sites also list major amenities, such as a pool or gym, but you may need to call ahead to find out about offerings such as whether or not hair dryers are provided.

- Inquire about business rooms or club floors. A business room will usually be equipped with a work center (comfortable desk and chair), two-line phone, in-room fax and Internet hookup, and the extra charges for this type of room are generally minimal. Rooms on a club or executive floor command a higher rate (usually anywhere from $20 to $40 more) than regular rooms, but the additional perks can be quite considerable: Most hotels staff their executive floor with a a concierge for several hours each day. There is generally a lounge area or separate conference rooms that can be used for meetings; private check-in as well as early and late check-out are frequently offered, and complimentary breakfast may be an additional guest service, as well as free soft drinks, coffee and tea, and "courtesy" hors d'oeuvres later in the day. Free local calls, use of the fitness center, and in-room amenities such as triple sheeting, turn-down service, and bathrobes are all among the special services offered at various hotel sites.

- If the hotel does not have a club or business floor, inquire about what other office services are available on-site. Many hotels now have in-room faxes, two-line telephones, and high-speed Internet access. Copy machines, mail and package facilities, computers, and Internet hookups (if you're not traveling with your laptop) are frequently available through a business center in the hotel.

- Confirm that the hotel you're inquiring about is not undergoing any type of renovation. The operator may tell you that work going on in the parking garage won't bother you, but be very wary of staying in any place where construction is taking place.

- Ask what frequent flyer miles the hotel honors. If you can add to your mileage, be sure to do so.

- Check the Web site or ask about shuttle services to and from shopping areas or other parts of town. If you can avoid having to rent a car or get your car out of the garage, it will make your life easier.

- If you need to entertain clients, try to select a hotel where the restaurant is well-regarded. That way you can entertain right at the hotel, saving you time going and coming to another location.

- When making reservations at a hotel that is part of a chain, circumvent the central reservations 800 number and call the hotel location directly. Direct contact with the reservation manager may get you a better room. He or she might even fax you a floor plan. (A great room at a hotel you frequent regularly merits a thank-you note or even flowers to the person who helped you.)

- Discuss available package plans directly with the person at the hotel where you'll be staying. They may have special deals that are not available through the 800-number reservation service.

- Request a nonsmoking room if you don't smoke and ask that your room not be located by the ice machines or the elevators, the noisiest part of any hotel floor. Big convention hotels are so huge that you also don't want to be all the way at the end of the hall-way—-it can be a long walk to the elevator. Have a quick discussion with the person who is booking your room and see what she recommends; you may need to balance convenience and safety (the rooms closer to the center of the hotel) with quiet (the rooms farther away from the main elevators and services).

- If you're staying in a motel, ask that your room door be on a hall-way, not opening directly to the parking lot.

- Getting directions off one of the general Internet "map" sites is a good way to find out how to get somewhere, but the best method is pulling directions directly from a hotel Web site or calling ahead for in-person advice. There may be some tricks, secrets, or "easiest ways" advice that the hotel personnel can offer you.

FREQUENT TRAVEL, SAME CITY

Loyalty to one hotel can make your life easier by letting you become familiar with one location. Over time you will find ways to make your stay very pleasant because the environment will be one with which you are comfortable.

- Befriend the staff. Take time to learn the names of those you see most frequently. You'll get first-rate service if they feel they know you.

- While it's nice to be warmly greeted by the same doorman or bellman, make a point of introducing yourself to the manager or the concierge. When you need tickets to a concert or some extra chairs brought to your room for a meeting, it's helpful to be able to deal with people who are familiar to you.

- Ask if the hotel has a package room where a few of your items can be stored. Leaving a bag with your gym equipment, an umbrella, extra shoes, and anything bulky that you need every time you travel can make packing much easier.

THE FRONT DESK

The person at the front desk holds your fate in his or her hands. He can upgrade you, improve the location of the room assigned you, or, if he's in a bad frame of mind, suddenly discover that all the better rooms are occupied. For that reason, politeness and respect are the order of the day when you check in.

- If a member of the staff says your room number aloud when summoning the bellhop, return to the front desk and request another room. For security reasons, it's important that your room number be kept private.

- Both men and women should use only a first initial when registering to keep anyone from knowing your full identity. In this way, your home can't be located when you're not there.

- If you check in late and the hotel doesn't have bellhops, ask if someone from the security department will see you to your room.

- Even if the front desk offers a "key" service when you go out, always keep yours with you to minimize the risk of anyone extra (beyond housekeeping) entering your room when you're not there.

THE ROOM

- Before you unpack, check the room:
  - Is the mattress firm without being rock hard? It's difficult to get a good night's sleep if the mattress dips in to a hollow in the middle.
  - Is the room clean?
  - Do the lights you need work properly?
  - How is the bathroom?
  - Consider safety: Check locks on the door, windows, and any balcony or patio door.
- If you don't like your room, call the front desk. Because of no-shows and early departures, hotels can often make last-minute changes.
- If the room is basically satisfactory but needs a few changes, don't be shy. By asking, you may be able to get:
  - A stronger lightbulb to replace the dim lightbulbs frequently used in hotel rooms.
  - A phone with a longer cord, or a remote phone, if yours doesn't reach as far as you need it to.
  - Extra toiletries.

- — Extra towels and blankets.
- — Smaller, larger, or softer pillows.
- — A board slipped under the mattress to create a bed with more support.
- If the room is acceptable, note the escape route you would take in case of fire.

N-ROOM TIPS

- Hotel telephone charges can really mount up. When you arrive, ask about the charge for Internet connection calls and ask how the other phone rate charges run. Many even charge for 800-number calls. If the hotel does not charge for local calls, you can save money by dialing out on the local line and then using the 800 number.

- Don't ever take a chance with your valuables and don't ever leave them "hidden" in your suitcase. Travel with as little as possible, and use the in-room safe or the downstairs vault to have money or jewelry or tickets locked up when you're not in the room. Some hotels will not be responsible for the in-room safe; they will only insure what is placed in the hotel vault. The chance of recovering stolen items is very low, and having to file reports and replace what is stolen will shift the focus away from the purpose of your trip, delaying your return home.

- Travel with a rubber doorstop. If you're concerned about hotel security, wedge the doorstop under your hotel room door. No one will be able to come in, even with a key, but keep in mind that in an emergency (a fire or medical problem that might keep you from getting to the door) emergency personnel won't be able to get to you either. Some people use a travel alarm in the same way. These look just like doorstops. They not only prevent entry into the room but they sound an alarm if there is the pressure of someone trying to open the door. These can be purchased at a travel shop.

- Some hotels equip each room with an iron and ironing board. If you check in and discover you don't have one, call upon your arrival. That way you're not waiting around the next morning for the iron to arrive if you need to press out your clothing.

- Dewrinkle clothes by hanging anything that is wrinkled on the shower rod. Close the bathroom door and run the shower long enough to steam up the room. Your clothes may smooth out so that you won't need to iron.

- Preorder room service breakfast if you plan to eat in your room. Plan out your morning prep time so that you can specify a time and know that you won't be in the shower when it arrives. Some businesspeople request that it arrive right after their wake-up call. If they've accidentally fallen asleep again, the arrival of breakfast assures that they are up. If you order it to arrive just after your shower, it may help you move a little faster.

- If you use the hotel "hang tag" to order breakfast the night before, women should use a last name only or a last name and first initial.

- Always check the hotel alarm clock (as well as your own if you travel with one), and be certain it isn't turned on. Otherwise, you may wake at the time the last guest had to get up.

- Be sure windows and doors are locked before leaving the room or going to bed.

- For security reasons, use your DO NOT DISTURB sign and turn on the television when you're out of the room and no longer need maid service.

- If a repair person comes to your room asking for access to do some repairs, call the front desk to verify that the person is legitimate. If you must let someone in, remain aware of what the person is doing, and stay between where that person is and the door of the room, so that you have access to getting out quickly if necessary.

TAKE NOTES

- Use an index card system or your personal digital assistant to write down comments about where you stay. Note the amenities available, the number of your favorite room, names of helpful staff members, area restaurants, and any other details you would like to know when you return.

- In a file folder, labeled for the town you've visited, keep your comments about where you stayed, directions to the hotel, brochures, business cards, and other items you'd like to be able to put your hands on prior to your next visit.

By befriending hotel personnel, newsstand clerks, and staff in nearby restaurants, it also makes you feel less isolated while away.

KEEP IT SIMPLE

1. Select a convenient hotel that offers helpful guest services such as on-premises office facilities as well as a good fitness center.

2. Treat the hotel staff courteously, and you'll improve your chance of getting the best room and services the hotel has to offer.

3. Always keep security issues in mind when staying in a hotel. Place valuables in the hotel vault instead of leaving them in your room; select a room that is quiet but not so out of the way; keep doors and windows locked; and be aware of your surroundings when you move about the hotel.

12

MAINTAINING YOUR SANITY WHILE ON THE ROAD

WHAT'S AHEAD

Smoothing the Way
Frustration Buffers
Just for You

I f you have a job that involves business travel, then the best way to manage your life is to consider your trips as part of life's adventure, an interesting way to do new things and meet new people.

Business travelers who look forward to doing things they don't have time to do at home or those who pursue hobbies while on the road (visiting used bookstores, collecting antiques) are best prepared to cope with the inevitable frustrations—the flight delays, the bad traffic, the client who doesn't show up at the agreed-upon time. You know all about that part of business travel; what you need to remember now is how to make the best of it.

Another key element to maintaining your sanity while on the road involves being certain to take time for yourself, just as you would if you were home. (You may actually have even more time for self-indulgence while traveling.)

"When I'm on the road, I divide my free time into thirds—I spend one third of it doing business work so that I don't have it to do when I return home; I spend one third keeping up with friends and family; and I always devote one third to doing something for me," says one businessperson. "Traveling is tiring and frustrating, and I feel like I deserve to treat myself particularly well on the road."

Here are some ideas for making business travel as pleasant as possible:

SMOOTHING THE WAY

- As you travel, treat others well, even the irritating ones. You'll find that a polite, respectful attitude may mean that you're the one who gets the special favors when there are not many tables left at the restaurant or when only two more passengers are boarding an otherwise full flight.

- Avoid angry confrontations at all costs. If something has really gone wrong, a letter to management on your business letterhead may get you an apology, discount coupons, or a free dinner, depending on the nature of the business where you had the unpleasant experience. Yelling at the employees will only raise your own blood pressure and make them unwilling to solve your problem.

FRUSTRATION BUFFERS

When things start going wrong (flight delays, traffic problems), concentrate on the big picture rather than the "small stuff."

"We were stuck in the Richmond airport for a three-hour delay, and I watched as people really fumed," says one traveler. "It doesn't do any good, because you're at the mercy of the weather and the airlines. About all you can do is find the best way possible to amuse yourself. I've read lots of good books waiting in airports, and the new data ports for plugging in laptops are lifesavers."

In addition to remaining calm, try to stay in control of incoming information. When you learn how serious the problem is you can begin to reset your priorities. Your destination airport may be shut down, but can you get into any other area airport?

Another frequent frustration has to do with appointments and traffic. Always remember to allow extra time for everything. That way you won't feel so upset if you're running late.

JUST FOR YOU

- Travel with a photo of your family or "significant other." Looking at the smiling faces of loved ones will remind you of what awaits you at home.

- Be sure you have a good haircut that adapts to climate changes. If you feel you look good, you'll feel better.

- Take along comfortable clothes to wear in the hotel room. Knit pants or lightweight sweatpants and a shirt can roll neatly to fill in an empty corner of your suitcase, and you'll be glad to have something soft to put on in the evening without feeling you have to get ready for bed.

- Sweatsocks can double as slippers. They take up less space in the suitcase and will keep your feet warm.

- Build in the time to live life normally even when you're on the road. Check into your hotel but then think of something interesting to do that evening; whether it's meeting a friend after work, going to a movie, or having a massage in your room, look at your downtime as time to be used in the way you see fit.

- Always pick up a local newspaper. Doing business will be easier if you know what's happening locally, and you may get some ideas on interesting things to do or see while you're there.

- Other than any concerns about safety, you should have the confidence to undertake any aspect of your adventure on your own—dine at a five-star restaurant, buy tickets for the theater, go to a movie. Don't hesitate to do anything just because you don't have a travel companion.

- Check city Web sites for restaurants and lunch spots where women feel comfortable.

- If you're in a town where there is a college, take a walk on the campus. You'll almost certainly see fliers about interesting lectures and concerts you could attend.

- If there's a hot show in the town you'll be visiting, plan ahead and order tickets.

- If you're staying in a hotel with a concierge, he or she can likely get you a "tough" ticket or can find a way to get you into the sold-out championship basketball game. However, these professionals are "rewarded" for their service—the more special the service the higher the tips, which can range from $10 to $100. (The concierge will provide you with maps, directions, and local advice for free; it's the special treats that earn the big money.)

- Make each trip a learning experience. Enjoy the people whom you meet while working.

- Send friends and family funny note cards, just for the fun of it.

PAMPER YOURSELF

- Treat yourself well. During the time you would normally be cooking, cleaning, doing errands, fixing things around the house, or taking care of others:

  — Watch a movie without interruptions.

  — Keep a journal.

  — Finish the novel you've been reading.

  — Pursue a hobby, such as shopping for a particular style of painting, collector pens, or campaign memorabilia.

  — Investigate what sports you could pursue.

  — Get a facial.

  — Get a manicure.

  — Call a friend, or look up a friend in this location. You may find that it's easy to renew contact with old buddies if you keep mental tabs on who lives where.

  — Take a class. Some business travelers who visit one city regularly find that taking yoga or photography in an evening class is actually possible when you don't have to worry about family responsibilities. If you've got to be in town anyway, make the most of it.

— One woman who quilts buys fabric that reminds her of the area and is making a memory quilt that depicts all the places she visits.

— A businessman who travels to Chicago frequently takes an hour or so each trip to visit a new museum. A book on Chicago museums lets him read about what he'll see in advance, and he appreciates it more as a result.

- Order room service when you want a relaxing night in the room. Women are twice as likely as men to use room service and more than half of those queried by Wyndham Hotels referred to it as "fun" and "indulgent." For most, it certainly beats fixing dinner at home!

- Don't overindulge. Travel is often associated with great food, but business travelers will feel better (and look better, too) if they maintain eating habits similar to those they follow at home.

ADD FAMILY OR FRIENDS OR FUN TO YOUR TRIP

Rather than race home after a week of meetings, consider having family or a friend come in and join you for a few days. You can view your destination through different eyes if you get to visit it leisurely with other people.

With or without family or friends, look around the area to see if you might enjoy an interesting side trip. If you're doing business in Denver in March, why not stay for the weekend and go on to one of the area ski resorts?

SIMPLIFY

- Delegate whatever you can, both at the office and at home.
- Do chores on the road so that you don't have to ruin your weekends. One woman travels home with everything from shoes for herself to her child's school supplies. "When I'm on the road, I often have time to get errands done, and if I do, it's a few things less I have to do when I get home."

- Shop throughout the year for holiday gifts.
- Cancel magazines you don't have time to read.
- Staying organized on the home front will help to maintain your sanity on the road. Save time by:
  — Keeping clutter at a minimum.
  — Shopping by mail or on the Internet.
  — Having groceries delivered.
  — Keeping a well-stocked pantry and a decently stocked refrigerator. That way when you return from a trip you can stop to pick up a few fresh items and not have to worry about having food at home.
  — Hiring additional help, whether it's someone to water plants or do heavy-duty cleaning for you, creates a support system.

PERSONAL TIME-SAVERS

- Come up with a hairstyle that is fast and easy.
- Work out an easy makeup routine.
- Plan outfits that coordinate with the same shoes and accessories.
- Turn your packing routine into a system by establishing a set pattern for what you pack and how you pack it.

- Write checklists and update them each trip.
- Always carry a list of telephone numbers for that particular trip: the hotel, the airlines, the car rental company, the client whom you're visiting, etc.
- Carry plenty of singles to make tipping easy.
- Take only what you need and leave excess at home.

WHEN THE GOING GETS TOUGH

Some workers have had luck with asking for a temporary "leave of travel," a sabbatical from being on the road all the time. If your family is going through a difficult time, or if you've missed a good number of significant events recently, talk to your boss about whether you could have a month or two off with no travel. So much business is done by phone, by video conference, and by e-mail, you could probably afford to slow down for a few weeks and then pick up your schedule with renewed energy later.

KEEP IT SIMPLE

1. While everyone loses their temper now and then, try to take in stride what happens while traveling. You'll feel calmer as a result, and people will respond to you better if you remain reasonable throughout any difficult experience.

2. Use business travel as an opportunity to explore new cities and find interesting things to do.

3. Pamper yourself. Business travel is hard work, and you deserve to treat yourself well.

13

STAYING HEALTHY ON THE ROAD:

HEALTH AND FITNESS

WHAT'S AHEAD

Exercise
Eating Properly
To Your Good Health
Bring from Home
Medical Smarts
Popping Pills Properly

If you've ever tossed and turned with fever in a hotel bed or used up every tissue in the room with a bad cold, you know how terrible it is to be sick while traveling. Or perhaps you've just felt sluggish and tired the whole time you were away.

Taking good care of yourself while you're traveling is absolutely vital to tolerating the stress that goes with business travel. Four aspects of maintaining good health on the road will be addressed in this chapter:

1. Getting exercise.

2. Eating properly.

3. Remaining as germ-free as possible.

4. Medical smarts.

The fifth aspect to maintaining good health is getting enough sleep, something that is exceedingly difficult to do while traveling. It will be discussed in the following chapter.

EXERCISE

- Even when you're on the road, try to get some form of aerobic exercise five days a week, at least 30 minutes each time. Exercise helps maintain a strong immune system, builds strength, and helps you maintain energy despite the stress of traveling.

- Select your hotel based on whether or not they have exercise facilities. Some hotels may call their equipment a "gym" or a "spa," but you may find that they are woefully inadequate. (A single treadmill and a StairMaster won't go far in serving a hotel full of businesspeople.) Ask what type of equipment they have, the size of the facility, and the hours of operation. If the gym isn't open during hours when you can get there conveniently, then see if there aren't other hotels in the area with better facilities.

- If your hotel does not have exercise facilities, ask if they have a reciprocal relationship with a gym in the area.

- If you belong to a health club at home, ask if they have a "sister" club in the city you're visiting. You may find your membership card will be accepted elsewhere.

- Ask at the front desk if the hotel has a map that shows a route for joggers. Run well before dark, preferably with a business colleague. (If the area looks at all questionable, forego outdoor exercise.) On one trip I found that with every block I ran I was getting deeper into questionable territory. After that I decided that I would participate in another form of exercise from then on!

- Exercise in the room before going to your meetings. A trainer at your home facility could provide you with a set of exercises to be done in the room in the morning, or if you flip through the television channels you may find an exercise program to follow.

- If you travel to one town consistently, investigate whether or not there are nearby exercise studios, and inquire about their class offerings. You may find that the yoga class you never have time to take at home is something you can fit in while on the road.

- Create your own exercise. In the airport, walk instead of taking the "people mover." Take the stairs instead of the escalator. Use your briefcase like a dumbbell, switching hands to exercise both sides of the body equally. You can create quite a workout for yourself simply by avoiding escalators and elevators and by walking briskly.

- What to do about exercising when you're sick? If your symptoms are in the neck or above (head cold or sore throat), do as much as you feel like. If your symptoms are below the neck (the chest, the stomach), don't exercise until you feel better. But most important, listen to your body. If you push yourself, it may zap your energy, leaving you feeling worse and having to spend more time recovering.

EATING PROPERLY

A big problem with business travel and eating is the fact that you lose control of your schedule. Instead of eating lunch at 1 P.M. when you're hungry, your plane may be delayed or your meetings may run late, and suddenly lunch is being presented to you at 2:30 P.M.—way too late in the opinion of your stomach. When you're famished, you either eat too much or nothing at all—neither of which is good for your body.

- Both alcohol and caffeine increase the dehydrating effect of air travel, so stay with juices and water when flying.

- If you choose to drink alcohol while traveling, do so only in moderation. Travel, particularly to different time zones, can be quite disorienting for your body. That and the additional fatigue can make the effect of alcohol more potent than when you're at home and relaxed.

- Drink plenty of water. This is easier to accomplish if you carry a water bottle with you.

- Eat wisely throughout the trip. While indulging in a big thick steak or a luscious dessert may seem like a good idea at the time you order it, a big meal slows your digestion and, particularly if you're attending a conference, becomes one more large meal in addition to all the heavy meals provided by the meeting organizers.

- To deal with an erratic eating schedule, carry high-energy snacks with you and eat smaller meals, supplemented by snacks as necessary, or travel with some soup packets and a hot water infuser (cup-size water warmer for travel, available in travel stores). If you miss a meal, you have a quick way to heat up a light snack in the room.

- Just because you're tired, don't increase your caffeine intake. If you're feeling groggy go for a brisk walk or sneak up to your room for a 15-minute power nap. (If you carry your own alarm clock, it's easy to set it to wake you in just a few minutes.) If neither of these options is available to you, stand up and move to the back of the room where you can stretch a bit to wake yourself up.

TO YOUR GOOD HEALTH

Inevitably, travel brings with it exposure to a host of germs we could have missed if we had stayed home. The recirculated air on planes is frequently given blame for illnesses. Even if you're not flying, when you travel you visit parts of the country where you are exposed to viruses that are of a different strain than those you are exposed to at home. Any tolerance you have built up to "home" germs is ineffective, and your resistance is further eroded by the wear and tear of travel.

Yet there are ways to minimize the effect of exposure. The first step, of course, involves maintaining general good health and getting enough sleep. The second involves doing what you can to avoid excessive exposure to germs:

- A benefit to traveling in colder weather is that your gloves protect you from excess cold as well as exposure to germs. Wear them as often as you can when it's cold. Subway straphangers and anyone touching public door handles have nothing to worry about when wearing woolen gloves!

- Wash hands as frequently as possible when traveling. Scrub them thoroughly with soap and warm water before meals, and if you've been introduced to and shaken hands with someone whom you later realize had a cold, remember to wash as soon as possible.

- Try to avoid touching your face or mouth. The mucous membranes of your nose, eyes, and mouth are easy entry points for germs and viruses.

- Travel with antibacterial hand wipes to stay as clean as possible when you can't wash up properly.

- In a hotel room, the bedspread will be the one part of the bed that is exposed to many people and yet not cleaned regularly. Remove it from the bed when you're ready to sleep. (While blankets aren't washed regularly either, because they tend to be sandwiched between the sheet and the bedspread, they aren't as exposed to germs as an outer bed covering. The most protected blankets are those that have a sheet on both top and bottom.)

BRING FROM HOME

- Always have your medical insurance information with you.

- Also have with you the names and telephone numbers of any prescribing doctors (or the general practitioner whom you see). A quick phone call to a doctor at home to ask a question may save you a medical visit while you're away.

- Carry a list of all medications (over the counter as well as prescriptions) you take. If you have to see a doctor while away, this information will be important. Don't rely on your memory when you're not feeling well.

- Have photocopies of drug prescriptions with you.

MEDICAL SMARTS

- If you have a chronic condition, wear an identification bracelet that provides information about your illness.

- If traveling overseas, be sure to get the required immunizations. Contact the Centers for Disease Control (*www.cdc.gov*) or call your local health department (travel medicine services department) for information.

- Make sure your tetanus protection is up to date. Adults should have a shot every ten years.

- Get a flu shot each fall. The new vaccinations don't give you a "touch of the flu" the way the old ones did. It's a good way to beef up your immune system even if you're not yet in the target group of those over 65.

- Many people swear by vitamin supplements. Since travel makes it difficult to be sure you're getting all the vitamins you need, try taking a multivitamin. If you want to tailor your vitamin dosages beyond this, check with your doctor or a qualified, certified nutritionist.

- If you have allergies, check with your doctor about managing them when you travel. Your allergic reaction will vary depending on the area you visit. You may need to increase your dosage, or you may be able to be medicine-free while away.

- If the timing of taking medication is critical, discuss with your doctor how to handle time zone changes.

- Don't put medicines in luggage that is checked through an airline. Keep it with you at all times.

- Consider heat exposure. (In a car, the glove compartment and trunk are poor storage spots because of temperature extremes.) Some medicines need to be kept cool. For a car trip, a cooler will help keep the medicine from warming up. On a plane, use a freezer pack and wrap the pack and the medicine in a plastic bag. If it's a long flight, ask the flight attendant about storing it in the plane's refrigerator.

- Once in the hotel room, consider where to store your medicine. Try to avoid keeping it in the bathroom where it is exposed to additional heat and humidity.

POPPING PILLS PROPERLY

- Review any warnings given on your medicines. Some make you more sensitive to sun or to heat.

- If you're trying a new medicine (prescription or over the counter), read the instructions carefully. If you have any questions regarding the use of the medicine or how it combines with other medicines you are taking, check with the pharmacist or call your doctor.

- If the packaging for over-the-counter medications is excessively bulky, take the pills out of the box, snip off the directions, and repackage everything together in a Ziploc plastic bag.

- Even if you use a pill dispenser for your prescription medicine, travel with pills in the original bottles. That way you have the information you need (medicine name, dosage, instructions, warnings, etc.) with you if another doctor asks about the prescription.

- If you need to take your medications with milk or with food, think ahead about how you will arrange this. For a car trip you can easily pack a cooler with what you need; if traveling by air, you may need to carry food with you or remember to order milk on the plane.

- If you're not feeling well, don't beg a doctor to give you antibiotics. Antibiotics don't work on many of the diseases we acquire, and more and more germs are becoming resistant because antibiotics have been overprescribed. Wait a day or two and use over-the-counter remedies until you have a better sense of what you're suffering from.

- *Never* take medication casually while traveling, and try to avoid taking anything in the middle of the night. No matter how awake you are, your surroundings are different, and it's too easy to make a mistake even with your most familiar medications. One woman accidentally took a sleeping pill after breakfast, and spent the rest of the day fighting off fatigue. If you have to take medicine in the middle of the night, get up out of bed, turn on the light, and be very careful about what you take under these less-than-alert conditions. That is your best hope for fully concentrating on exactly what it is you are taking.

KEEP IT SIMPLE

1. Be sure to work exercise into your travel days. Getting your body moving will let you stretch out the kinks in your muscles from traveling, and you'll feel better in general by maintaining an exercise routine.

2. Wash your hands frequently while traveling. Establishing this

habit will make a big difference in your ability to stay well on the road.

3. If you have any concerns about taking medications while you're away, check with your doctor.

14

STAYING HEALTHY ON THE ROAD:

SLEEP

WHAT'S AHEAD

Advance Planning
The Peaceful Body
A Good Sleep Environment
Your Evening Routine

189

In a strange town for a corporate job I'd been hired to do, I checked into the motel where the company had made reservations for me. The accommodations weren't great, but I thought, "Well, how bad could it be? It's only one night . . ."

About 9:30 P.M. that evening, I found out how bad it could be when a group of businesspeople returned and started partying in the rooms all around me. Despite a call to the motel operator, the party continued, and I barely slept a wink. The next morning when I had to give my presentation, I felt like a zombie.

From that night forth, I've always insisted on the right to approve accommodations in advance. If the place is too small for me to be able to move rooms if necessary, then I ask to be booked at a larger chain where there is some quality control. A well-known operation will likely have walls that are a bit thicker and because of better management, my call to the operator might have been heeded.

When Westin Hotels conducted a sleep study, they found that 63 percent of travelers consider a good night's sleep the most important service a hotel can provide. However, 50 percent of executives surveyed said they slept worse on the road and three quarters of them reported needing to catch up on sleep when they returned home.

Late meetings and early breakfasts make it difficult to have a leisurely sleep, but to avoid being groggy and unproductive for the next day's undertakings, it's important to do what you can to get a good night's rest.

ADVANCE PLANNING

- Take along an eyeshade and earplugs. If a room can't be fully darkened, the eyeshades will aid in sleeping; the earplugs can be invaluable on a morning when you don't need to be awakened by a wake-up call or an alarm.

- If you have back or neck problems, pack your chiropractic pillow. There's no sense in enduring additional pain while you're on the road.

- Travel with a good book or your favorite magazine. Reading just before going to bed is calming and gets your mind off work and missing your family.

- Try to keep your morning and evening routines similar to what you do at home. If you exercise and then shower at home, then do that while traveling. And if at home you select and lay out your clothing for the next morning, then do so now. Maintaining a routine will keep you in a better rhythm for the day.

THE PEACEFUL BODY

- Avoid caffeine after 5 P.M., and consume alcohol in moderation. Coffee, tea, and caffeine-containing soft drinks are all stimulants, and despite the temporary calm provided by alcohol, drinking is not conducive to good sleep. In a survey conducted by Hilton Hotels and the Sleep Foundation, it was found that business travelers actually report drinking 25 percent more alcohol and consuming 25 percent more caffeine while on the road—exactly the wrong things to do.

- Even if you are on an expense account, forget the steak and the rich dessert. Rich foods won't help you sleep. Order lightly, or if you're at a dinner with a set menu, focus on the soup, salad, and vegetables.

- If chocolates on the pillow are among the hotel's amenities, set yours aside for a pick-me-up later the next day (again, not after 5 P.M.), or take them home to your kids—a sure winner. The caffeine in the chocolate stimulates your system and won't lead to a relaxed night.

- A perfect form of exercise for after dinner is a walk; a heavy workout at the gym right before bed will be too stimulating.

A GOOD SLEEP ENVIRONMENT

- Create a good sleeping environment in your hotel room. Some hotels have "white noise" machines to drown out other sounds, and if yours does, use it.

- If the drapes aren't already closed, do so when you get to the room.

- A cooler room temperature is more conducive to sleep, so check the thermostat and turn it down if necessary.

- Put in a wake-up call for the next morning so that once you do go to sleep you needn't worry about being wakened in time. To be safe, set your travel alarm as a backup.

- Put the DO NOT DISTURB sign on the door and turn off your cell phone.

YOUR EVENING ROUTINE

- Review your schedule for tomorrow, updating it as needed.

- Phone home if you have promised that you will. Try to do this earlier in the evening, perhaps before dinner if you can. If you do it at the end of the evening and learn there are problems at home, your phone call may be stressful, and that won't be conducive to a good night's sleep.

- If you're spending the evening in the room, then by all means check e-mail and voice mail. You may be able to take care of a few issues before tomorrow. However, if it's late, try to avoid checking office communication systems or do so briefly, saving nonpriority items for the next day. Any type of stimulation may make it more difficult for you to unwind.

- Don't do anything too interesting right before bed. If you become mentally engaged in something, your adrenaline will start flowing and you'll soon find it harder to go to sleep.

- Pamper yourself. Order room service and rent an in-room movie. A bubble bath, aromatherapy, or a manicure are the types of things women travelers may decide makes travel time more enjoyable.

- If you've been out for the evening and return to your room late, you still need to build in some time to relax before going to bed. (If you collapse into bed, your sleep won't be as restful.)

- Shower or take a warm bath to relax.

- Get into bed and read for a few minutes. Watching television is fine if you set a limit. Some people get involved in a late-night movie and the time gets away from them.

- Do isometrics when you first lie down. Start with your feet and legs and go all the way up your body, tightening and relaxing the muscles in sequence. Afterward, your body will feel more relaxed and some of the day's tension will be gone.

- The National Sleep Foundation reports that worrying about getting enough sleep actually causes insomnia in travelers. If you wake during the night, don't worry. Distract yourself. If you've got a good novel or a favorite magazine, turn on your bedside light and read for 15 to 20 minutes. You'll soon be ready to go back to sleep.

KEEP IT SIMPLE

1. Try to maintain the routine you follow at home. This will help you sleep more normally.

2. Plan to have some quiet time in the room before going to bed. Your body needs the opportunity to relax and unwind.

3. If you do wake up during the night, read something mindless for 15 minutes or so. Don't work or think about the day ahead, and chances are good that you'll be able to go back to sleep.

15

TRAVEL
SECURITY

WHAT'S AHEAD

Before You Go
Advance Planning About Luggage
Don't Take Your Eyes Off Your Laptop!
Safety Awareness
In Transit

"I realized what was happening as the fellow bumped into me, but by the time I grabbed for my wallet it was too late . . ."

"I put my laptop on the airport security conveyor belt, and that was the last I saw of it."

"I'm only going down to swim a few laps. I'll slip my wallet into that special section of my suitcase . . . No one will ever know . . ."

Don't let the words "I should have known better" cross your lips when traveling.

Unfortunately for you, business travelers make good targets for thieves. Businesspeople are likely to be carrying cash, laptops, and other valuables, and they are often in a hurry and easily distracted because of the stress of traveling. What's more, a person traveling on business is unlikely to risk missing a flight to report a crime or to make a return trip to serve as a witness.

With some planning and a general sense of awareness, you and your possessions can have safe passage until you are back home. Here's what to do:

BEFORE YOU GO

- Clean out your briefcase, wallet, and purse, removing things you don't really need. Leave at home extra credit cards such as those for local establishments and various "club" cards, while keeping major bank cards, your driver's license (you'll need it for identification even if you're not planning to drive), and any health and medical insurance cards. If anything is stolen, you will have less to replace.

- Photocopy all credit cards, your driver's license, and the front pages of your passport. Leave one copy with a family member or a co-worker whom you trust. Take the other with you, but keep it in your suitcase, not in your purse or briefcase.

- Prepare a short list of emergency information and get the card laminated. (You can use the card again and again if it's plasticized so it will last for a long time.) List credit card cancellation numbers, your corporate travel department emergency number, your airline reservation number, frequent flyer numbers, and passport number. Don't put it in your wallet. Once you're at your destination, store it in the hotel safe.

- Spread out your money so that it isn't all in one place. If you lose some, you won't be totally wiped out. It's helpful to have single dollar bills easily accessible for tips; that way you won't reveal where you're carrying your billfold when all you need is a dollar.

- Don't carry your wallet in your back pocket. Men should put their wallet in their inside jacket pocket, or use a money clip and carry their bills in their front pants pocket. Or consider using a money belt if you're carrying a lot of extra cash. If you're uncomfortable changing your habits and really want to carry your wallet in your back pocket, put one or two large (one-quarter-inch-width) rubber bands around it. Because the bands prevent the wallet from sliding out easily, it is almost impossible for someone to quickly tug a wallet out of your pocket unnoticed. While it will also take you longer to extract your wallet in order to pay for purchases, this is a minor inconvenience compared to the possibility of being robbed.

- Travel with very few valuables. Those you take should be worn or stored in your carry-on bag, not your luggage.

- Always travel with a small flashlight. It can come in handy in a parking garage or if your hotel experiences a blackout.

- When you're driving, don't let the gas tank go under the quarter-tank mark. In unfamiliar territory, you won't know where the next gas station is, and for both business and security reasons, you want to be sure you can always keep going until *you* decide it's time to stop.

ADVANCE PLANNING ABOUT LUGGAGE

- Skip the designer luggage. From a crime standpoint, the act of carrying something expensive already sets you apart from the crowd.

- Don't take too much luggage. You'll be overwhelmed simply moving from place to place, and this will make you a potential victim.

- For luggage tags and any other type of travel identification, use your business address and phone number. If the airlines are trying to reach you about a lost bag it won't help to call you at home.

- Be sure you have identification inside your bags as well as outside. If the tag gets ripped off the exterior, you want someone to have another way to locate you.

- Remove old flight tags from luggage to avoid confusion. Secure your luggage with a good lock, available at luggage or travel shops.

- Keep in physical contact with your luggage at all times. Put it between your legs while waiting at airports or in hotel lobbies, and in the bathroom, tote bags may fit on the shelves in the stall. If not, keep the luggage away from the front of the stall where it could be grabbed. (Don't hang your purse on the hook in the stall; use the shelf or keep it right by you.)

- Keep a separate record of what is in your luggage.

- Don't accept luggage help unless the person is in uniform.

DON'T TAKE YOUR EYES OFF YOUR LAPTOP!

More than three hundred thousand laptop computers are stolen from offices, hotels, and airports (in that order) each year, and part of it is due to careless handling on the part of the owner. People who wouldn't dream of leaving a purse or their wallet unattended in an airport *have* left their laptop and luggage out in plain view while making a phone call or visiting the men's or ladies' room. Here's what to do to protect yours:

- Insure your laptop. If your company doesn't provide insurance, buy it yourself. It's worth it.

- Be sure to always have a backup of what is on your laptop. If you're traveling with sensitive information, it should be encrypted.

- Tape your business card to the bottom of the laptop, and have your driver's license number (not your Social Security number) engraved on the case. You should also program your computer so that the opening screen identifies you as the owner and provides information on how you can be reached.

- Install a laptop alarm or a software device such as CompuTrace, which instructs the computer to "phone home" to report its whereabouts. The police can take it from there.

- Don't pack your laptop in a bag that is to be checked. Those bags take a beating, and if the bag should be opened, your laptop will be gone in an instant.

- Don't carry a laptop in a case with a manufacturer's logo. Use a generic case.

- Keep your hands or eyes on your laptop at all times. When you reach airport security, hold on to your laptop until you're about to walk through the metal detector. A classic airport scam is to steal purses and laptops coming off the security conveyor belt. (If the person just ahead is participating in the scam and creates a delay, it can be a long time before you're reunited with your possessions.)

- Put your laptop at your feet on the plane. A laptop can die an instant death if it falls from an overhead bin when someone else rearranges the bin's holdings.

SAFETY AWARENESS

- Leave yourself enough time so that you aren't overly anxious.

- Map out your route, and if you're unsure, double-check it with the concierge or anyone who lives locally. You can't afford to get lost in an unfamiliar place.

- Always remain alert to your surroundings when leaving your room, walking on the street, jogging, or going to your car. Know who is around you and what they are doing.

- Look and act confident. You want to seem as though you are someone who knows where he or she is going.

- Avoid isolated areas. Stay on well-lighted streets.

- Never volunteer that you're traveling alone, and if you are walking alone and become nervous, blend in with a group and act like you're with them.

- Have your keys out and ready to use as you approach your car or room.

- In a dark parking lot, ask someone to see you to the car.

- Many crimes happen at pay phones. If you have to stop to use one, face outward while making your call, stay alert, hang onto your belongings, and avoid isolated phone booths and ones without lights.

- Thieves and pickpockets often work in teams where one will distract a victim while the other one robs him or her. If you find yourself in the midst of any type of hubbub, hold on to your purse or wallet.

- Wherever you are—hotel conference center, someone else's office, your hotel room—locate exits in case you have to get out in case of fire.

N TRANSIT

- At the airport, double-check the tags placed on your luggage to be certain the bags are going where you are.

- If you're on a flight that arrives after dark, prearrange for a car service to pick you up at the airport or try to take the shuttle. Don't rent a car and risk driving in a new city at night when you're tired and could get lost. You can pick up a car in town once you're there.

- Rental cars should have in-state plates. Out-of-state plates make you a possible victim.

- Keep your car locked while you're in and out.

- Lock valuables in the trunk.

- Put tourist signs (maps, guidebooks, etc.) in the glove compartment so you don't look like a tourist.

- If a cab driver makes you uneasy, use your cell phone to pretend to call someone and give an estimated arrival time at your hotel and mention the cab number.

- Never leave behind items with your mailing address (magazines) on planes or at restaurants or hotels. (It provides someone with your address, and because you're there, it means your home may be unattended.) You can toss the publication, just remove the part of the cover where the mailing label appears and rip it up separately.

- To keep current on security issues, visit the National Business Travel Association's Web site: *www.biztraveler.org*.

KEEP IT SIMPLE

1. Carry only your necessary credit cards and documentation, and make photocopies of those items so that if they have to be

replaced you have the information you need. (Keep one with you and leave one with a family member or co-worker.)

2. Spread your money out and carry it in different places so if you are robbed, you don't lose all the cash that you've got with you.

3. Don't become casual about safety. It's important to remain alert and aware wherever you are, but particularly when you're traveling.

16

BUSINESS
TRAVEL TO
FOREIGN
COUNTRIES

WHAT'S AHEAD

Watch the Expiration Date on Your Passport
To Your Continued Good Health
Use the Internet

Doing business in China, South Africa, Tunisia, or France are all very different experiences; however, there are some basic guidelines that can help you prepare for foreign travel in general.

In addition to following the advice in this chapter, review the chapters on jet lag and staying healthy. Jetting through 6, 8, 10, and 12 time zones is hard on your body, yet business travelers are often expected to arrive, conduct business, and come back within a few days. For that reason, anything you can do to manage jet lag and eat and sleep well will be very helpful to you in taking care of yourself and your business.

WATCH THE EXPIRATION DATE ON YOUR PASSPORT

There are few things more annoying than beginning to plan for an overseas trip and realizing that your passport is about to expire:

- Renewal by mail will take about 25 days, but you've got to allow time for snafus. Start the renewal process six months in advance of when your passport expires. For an application form, log on to *www.travel.state.gov*.

- If you must leave for a trip and have let your passport expire, call a regional passport office for an emergency appointment. Take your airline tickets with you for proof of urgency.

- Always purchase your airline tickets in the same name as the one you use on your passport—no nicknames, no extra initials. Customs will be verifying your identity, so consistency is important.

TO YOUR CONTINUED GOOD HEALTH

- Be sure you have the required vaccinations for the countries you are visiting. Your doctor, travel agent, or the embassy can help you determine what you need. The Centers for Disease Control also has a number for questions regarding immunizations: 404–332–4559. For updates on current epidemics, contact the CDC at 404–639–3311.

- For any medications you take, obtain two prescription bottles to take with you, one for your carry-on luggage and the other to pack in your suitcase. If anything happens to either piece of luggage, you'll still have access to the medication you need.

- Before departure, get names of English-speaking, qualified medical personnel. For help, contact the International Association for Medical Assistance to Travelers: 716–754–4883.

- Check on your medical insurance. What would be covered and how quickly would the bill be paid if you were to get sick while away? If you were in a third world country, who would pay to evacuate you to a country with more sophisticated medical services?

- Keep a card with your doctor's name and contact information and a list of your medications and allergies with you at all times. (Laminate it so that it will last longer.)

USE THE INTERNET

- To obtain correct information regarding needed visas and other paperwork related to your trip, log on to *www.embassy.org*, which lists all the embassies in the Washington, D.C. area.

- How far will your money go? Check out the Universal Currency Converter (*www.xe.net/currency*), a Web site that provides the best bank exchange rates for local currency. You type in the amount of the currency you want to convert, and the site will tell you how much foreign money you will have. (You'll want to become skilled at making the conversion in your head. Once you're there and converting money in person, you need to calculate how much you expect to receive.)

- When traveling to foreign countries where you may prefer to pack rather than "purchase if necessary," taking time to check the weather will pay off in comfort and convenience. Since no one can truly predict exactly what weather will await you, the most helpful information is the average weather for the time of year you're traveling. The World Wide Climate (*www.worldclimate.com*) provides monthy-by-month summaries of temperature highs and lows as well as rainfall averages. If you learn you're traveling during the country's rainiest month, you'll know to be prepared. Check out the following weather websites for more information:

— The Weather Channel: *www.weather.com*.

— AccuWeather site: *www.accuweather.com*.

— One Web site provides a live video feed of weather at a particular location: *www.rainorshine.com*.

BE SURE TO TRAVEL WITH . . .

- A photocopy of your actual passport, two additional passport photos, proof of citizenship, necessary visas, your tickets, and your driver's license. Pack them separately from your originals. If you should lose any of these documents, you'll have fewer challenges to getting new ones if you have plenty of proof as to who you are and what you're trying to replace.
- Medical information (see above).
- The emergency assistance numbers for your credit card company and travel agency. Those numbers can be called collect for help on finding emergency medical and legal help in foreign countries.
- A list of contacts at the U.S. Embassy.
- Phone list of in-country corporate contacts.
- A map of the country.
- Dictionary.
- Extra cash in local currency.
- Women should always have a scarf when traveling internationally. It can be used to cover the head or shoulders when needed to observe local customs.

ADDITIONAL SECURITY PRECAUTIONS

- Get a consular information sheet for the countries you plan to visit. Contact the State Department or check the Web site.

- If staying abroad in one country for several weeks or more, register with your country's embassy or consulate.

- The U.S. Department of Transportation offers a recorded message providing information on security threats to transportation systems: 800–221–0673.

- For security concerns, check Hot Spots on the Web, a free travel intelligence service offered by Air Security International: *www.airsecurity.com*.

- For traveling in unstable areas of the world, check the State Department's Web site: (*http//htravel.state.gov/travelwarnings*), to find out whether a travel warning has been issued. You can also call 202-647-5225. This is also the number to call if you are a victim of a crime overseas.

- Leave a copy of your itinerary and a copy of your passport with someone in your office whom you can reach 24 hours a day.

- Leave valuables at home. Women should wear fake jewelry rather than anything of value. The last thing you want to occupy your time while traveling on business is the aggravation concerning lost or stolen goods.

- Get a money belt to wear inside your clothing for your passport, money, and plane tickets. The possible discomfort of wearing it will be outweighed by the knowledge that your money and passport are safe.

- A wedding ring on a woman will help safeguard against unwanted male attention in most foreign countries. Have with you an inexpensive band you can wear as needed.

PREPARING FOR YOUR TRIP

- In most countries (with the exception of third world countries), you should be able to use your bank card to withdraw currency from local ATM machines. Visit your bank and get the personal identification number (PIN) you'll need. This saves time because you needn't purchase travelers' checks before departure, and it often saves money: you usually get a better rate on the currency conversion.

- Learn the language and the customs. Check out a Web site like *dailylinguist.com*, a good site to learn languages. Go to *subscribe @dailylinguist.com*, and the site will send you a phrase a day.

- If you don't have time to learn the language, try to pick up a few phrases to show some effort in learning the local culture.

- Check out the small translators that will let you type in a word or phrase and it will present you digitally with the information you need.

- Research different customs. In some countries, women can't wear sleeveless dresses, shorts, or miniskirts.

- Learn about the holidays so that you don't arrive at the beginning of one.

- Find out what foreign phone and electrical adapters are needed and bring them with you.

- Get a miniworld band radio that lets you keep up to date on politics, weather, and sports without lugging a lot of heavy audio equipment. These radios receive AM, FM, and 6 shortwave bands of news and information and run on two AA batteries.

- Your cell phone won't work overseas most of the time, but you can rent one that will.

TRAVEL WISELY

- Be sure to check on dimensions for carry-on bags and luggage restrictions for your flight. International airlines tend to be quite specific about this.

- Porters can be very difficult to find in other countries, so it is more important than ever that you be able to manage your suitcase, your briefcase, and if applicable, a purse.

- If your bag is not on wheels, then invest in one of the collapsible luggage "dollies."

- If you need a carry-on bag in addition to your suitcase and briefcase, consider a backpack. While most business people would not want to be seen sporting around Paris with one, a backpack serves as a practical carry-on bag. Then you can leave it in your hotel for the rest of your stay.

- Use luggage tags on every piece, including carry-ons. Yarn, stickers, or a colored tab will be helpful in finding your bag on the luggage carrousel, or if you have a driver or are lucky enough to find a porter, the colored item will help both of you identify your bag.

- Inquire what items are available at the hotel. If the hotel provides a hairdryer and an iron, that's one less thing to worry about packing or taking the correct electrical adapters.

- Permanently pack a nylon rain jacket. At some point during your travels you're guaranteed to encounter wet, rainy weather.

- If you purchase anything while you're away, save time in Customs by packing all the new purchases in one bag and keeping all your receipts together.

- Travel in comfortable clothing. After a six-, eight-, or twelve-hour flight, your business clothing will be a mess if you fly in it. If there's any chance you'll have to go directly to a meeting, stop somewhere in the airport to freshen up and change.

- If you don't speak the language, pick up a brochure or a matchbook with the name of your hotel. If other forms of communication fail, you can present someone (a cab driver, a person trying to direct you on the street) with the brochure or matchbook, and they'll be better able to help you get back to your hotel.

WHILE AWAY

- If you have to leave your laptop at home and are visiting many locations and don't have an office "home base," look for cybercafes. At this writing, there are almost 3,000 of them in 117 countries. To access your mail easily, set up a free e-mail account with Hotmail or at Yahoo!, and program your regular Internet to forward your e-mail. If you have a local Internet service provider, this will permit you to access your mail without paying for a long-distance call.

KEEP IT SIMPLE

1. Travel with photocopies of important documents and leave a spare copy, along with your itinerary, with one of your co-workers.

2. Plan ahead in case of medical emergency. Know who to contact, and be sure you have a card that states relevant information about you.

3. Ingratiate yourself with those whom you're visiting on business by expressing interest in their culture and learning what you can of their language.

ABOUT THE AUTHORS

RONNI EISENBERG, author of *Organize Yourself!*, has given a multitude of workshops, lectures, and demonstrations across the country on how to get organized. She lives and works in Westport, Connecticut, with her husband and three children.

KATE KELLY, who co-authors Ronni's books, is a professional writer who owns and operates her own publishing business. She lives in Westchester County, New York, with her husband and three children.